Contents

GW00507367

Introduction

BREXIT, COVID 19 and the Stock Ma

General Points

Section 3. Purchasing Shares

****

Introduction

It is true to say that, for many years, the ownership of stocks and shares and the workings of the stock exchange were a mystery to most people. Shares and the stock exchange were seen to be a specialist areas dominated by the well heeled and, invariably, the old-school tie network. Times have changed and now share ownership is within everyone's grasp. This has been so because of changes in the ownership of former public utilities and the dispersing of shares to the ordinary person. Alongside that has come an opening up of the whole area of share dealing.

However, over the last few years we have seen some horror stories about the stock market and investors losing a lot of money. Some of these losses have been in mini-bond investments, i.e. the Woodford Funds and also London Capital and Finance and also in assorted other investments. This emphasises the fact that investing in stocks and shares can be very risky indeed and, rather than make money you can also lose money.

Today, following Britain's exit from the EU, The questions are what will happen to sterling; or to the UK economy, rather than the nitty-gritty of corporate activity. BREXIT may have a meaningful effect on the earnings and dividend payments for certain companies that depend on EU markets or supply chains. For others, the currency is a key issue. For dollar earners, a weak sterling flatters their income, while other areas struggle in relative terms because their income is in sterling. However, for most it is a sideshow in the day-to-day running of their businesses. Wait and see.

BREXIT, COVID 19 and the stock market

Over the last two years in the UK, 2020-2022, no two events have had a greater impact on stock market indices, including the FTSE 100, than Brexit and Covid-19. The FTSE 100 has either risen or fallen with almost every new Brexit and Covid-19 development as investors have speculated on what each one could mean for the economy and, most importantly, for their investments.

We need to look deeper into this to understand the swings we see in stock markets whenever there is significant news on either Covid-19 or Brexit.

BREXIT

Stock market indices like the FTSE 100 have shown significant sensitivity to Brexit news and headlines ever since the shock 2016 referendum result. On 24 June 2016, the day that the referendum results were announced, the FTSE 100 fell by 9%. Since then, other Brexit developments have been accompanied by swings in the FTSE 100 and other stock market indices.

For example, on 17 January 2017, when the then Prime Minister Theresa May announced plans for a potential 'hard' Brexit, the FTSE 100 fell by 1.5%. On 20 April 2020, it rose by 0.45% when Brexit talks resumed after a six-week interruption caused by Covid-19.

Most recently, on 15 October 2020, the FTSE 100 fell 1.8%. This was after Boris Johnson expressed disappointment about the progress of Brexit trade deal negotiations during a call with EU leaders. This understandably made investors anxious about the potential for a no-deal Brexit.

A week later, on 23 October, the FTSE 100 rose by 1.3% after talks about the deal resumed. We have now well passed the exit date, which was on 1st January 2021. However, the stock market has had no time to steady as a result of the pandemic.

Covid-19

Over the last two years, the impact of Covid-19 on the stock market has been even greater than that of Brexit. For example, on 12 March 2020, the blue chip index suffered its second biggest one-day crash in history and the largest since 1987 amid concerns over the spread of the virus. It then fell to its lowest value on 23 March 2020.

However, the index soon made a tentative recovery. This was after lockdown measures started to calm investors' concerns about the spread of the virus. More recently, following the second wave, and subsequent lockdown, due to rising Covid-19 cases, the FTSE 100 started to fall again. It ended up hitting a six-month low in late October 2020. But news of two promising vaccines from Pfizer and Moderna saw the FTSE 100 rally once again. It rose by 4.7%, or 276 points, after Pfizer's vaccine news. This, in effect, added close to £70bn to this index's value. The index rose by a further 1.6% after Moderna's announcement of its own vaccine news.

In a nutshell, positive news about Covid-19 usually translates to a gain in the FTSE 100. A vaccine, for example, signals to investors that normality, particularly in the business world, might resume soon. It suggests that companies' earnings could go back to pre-pandemic levels and that's it's therefore worth investing in them.

Conversely, negative news, like a rise in cases, points to an uncertain economic future causing investors to be extremely cautious.

How can stock market investors take advantage of Brexit and Covid-19 news?
Savvy investors know better than to base their investment strategy on trending news and headlines. There will always be forces like these that cause short-term ups and downs in the stock market.

The best approach is sticking to a long-term investment strategy that's based on your preferences and capabilities. Over the long term, the market has an upward bias. Those who are patient are often able to garner good returns from their investments.

With that said, negative reactions to Covid-19 and Brexit developments can provide a great opportunity for smart investors to buy stocks and shares at discounted prices.

While it's up to you to decide whether to pounce on this opportunity, remember the advice of Warren Buffett, one of the world's greatest investors: "Be fearful when others are greedy and greedy when others are fearful."

Short term investment trends-making a quick buck

Another area that has grown is that of the speculative investor looking for quick returns. Unless you really know what you are doing, then it pays to keep in mind that you are an investor and therefore should look carefully and spot those industries that will likely grow in the future and invest for the medium to ling term, balancing your portfolio to achieve that aim.

Get rich quick

If you have the knowledge, you can speculate and make money quick on the stock market. However, whatever you read, in most cases, the stock market is not generally a get rich quick scheme. It is a place to grow expertise, think in the long term and use your good judgment. As mentioned, try to visualise the future performance of companies, for example, a small investment in Amazon, Google, Apple and Tesla pre-pandemic will have quadrupled by 2022.

A word of warning

One of the world's most widely respected investors says that stock markets are out of touch with reality after their post-pandemic surge. Charlie Munger, the 97-year-old vice-chairman of Berkshire Hathaway and the right-hand man to Warren Buffett, the renowned billionaire stock-picker and dealmaker, said that the market was "even crazier" now than it was during dotcom boom of the late 1990s, which proceeded a crash. At a conference in Sydney, Munger said: "Some of the valuations we saw in the dotcom boom were higher, but overall I consider this as being even crazier than dotcom boom, which blew up in 2000."

On Wall Street the S&P 500 has doubled in value since last spring's crash. So far this year, in the United Sates, nearly $900 billion has been poured into equity funds, which, according to Bank of America, is more than in the previous 19 years put together. Munger said that many US stocks were trading on a price-to-earnings valuation of 35 times or more, well above historic levels. He and Buffett, 91, are known for searching Wall Street for stocks that they feel have been unfairly neglected by the wider market. However, he said it was becoming increasing difficult to find a solid business at a fair price. "You have to pay a great deal for good companies and that reduces your future returns," he said. He praised China's authorities, which have made moves this year to try to temper prices of everything from stocks to commodities to property. He said that the United States was "inferior to China" when it came to trying to rein in markets. "They're right to step out, step hard on booms and to not let them go too far. They're acting in a more adult fashion," he said. Munger also backed China's approach to cryptocurrencies, which he dislikes. "I wish they'd never been invented," he said. "Again I admire the Chinese, I think they made the correct decision, which was to simply ban them. In my country, English-speaking civilization has made the wrong decision, I just can't stand participating in these insane booms." He also questioned the intentions of cryptocurrency investors who, he said, were only "thinking about themselves ...Just look at them, I wouldn't want any one of them to marry into my family."

In short, be very careful when considering purchasing stocks. Beware of the 'quick buck'

Ethical Investing
What is ethical investing?
Ethical investing is when individual investors choose the assets and stocks, they will invest in based on their own ethical values and beliefs. This can range from excluding specific firms that operate in areas such as gambling, tobacco, adult entertainment, weapons or alcohol or by selecting funds that the consider a range of ethical factors and/or delivers positive ethical outcomes. Positive ethical outcomes can include social and environmental benefits.

How to invest ethically
Investors can choose their own investments, selecting stock in individual firms based on analysis of their ethical credentials. However, this is time consuming and requires regular research

to help make sure your choices remain relevant and offer a good return. A suitable investment fund includes a range of ethical investments based on a set of guiding principles or rules for managing the fund.

Investors can use an investment platform to choose, invest in and manage their ethical investments. One such platform is Tribe Impact Capital, a wealth management firm that offers investments in companies that work towards achieving the United Nations Sustainable Development Goals. https://tribeimpactcapital.com

Why invest ethically?

Making a choice to invest ethically is not only good for wider society and the environment but ethical investments have been shown to outperform the returns of their non-ethical equivalents. In July 2020 Moneyfacts revealed that 140 ethical unit trusts had grown by 4% in the 12-months to 1 July 2020 compared to a contraction of 1.5% for those not in the ethical category. For very good advice on ethical investing and recommendations of the best ethical investment funds go to: moneyfacts.co.uk/investments-how-to-invest-your-money/guides/ethical-investing.

Taking into account the numerous perils for the novice investor, this book is intended for anyone who wishes to understand more about the workings of the stock market and also the whole culture and environment of shares and share dealings before diving in.

Knowledge is the key to everything and it is the intention of this book to provide a comprehensive overview of how the stock market works, how companies work, how to go about buying and selling shares and also how to understand information relating to share performance. By discussing the nature of investments, the operations of companies, the stock market, the nature and costs of shares and also the interpretation of data in financial pages, this brief introduction to the stock market should provide enough information for the smaller investor to operate with confidence and to make informed decisions.

By investing carefully, taking time to analyse markets and regularly reading financial data, there is no reason why the small investor cannot prosper on the stock market.

****

SECTION 1

THE FACTORS THAT AN INVESTOR SHOULD TAKE INTO ACCOUNT

Ch. 1

The Individual Investor

Defining the 'investor'

Individual investors can be defined as people who, after meeting all their expenses from their income have a surplus left which they wish to invest, one way or another. There are many reasons for investing, the main one being to meet future needs. Investors can keep a cash reserve in a building society or bank, they can invest in something that they think will appreciate in value, such as property, or shares which can be resold when needed.

Purchasing assets

Assets come in many shapes and forms, cash, premium bonds, securities such as shares in a company or gilt-edged stocks (which are government issued bonds), life assurance policies, works of art, property and so on. Each type of asset has different characteristics which will appeal to different investors. The subject of this book is the stock market and therefore we will be discussing stocks and shares as a viable investment.

The first characteristic of an investment that needs to be considered is an annual return: does ownership of a particular commodity entitle the investor to receive any income and if that is the case, what is the level of that income?

Income can be realised in a number of ways. There is the good old fashioned deposit in a bank or building society, which will give a monthly quarterly or annual return but not at rates that will excite the adventurous investor, certainly not at the current time of writing, 2022, where rates have dropped to almost Zero in some cases. However, these may pick up a little following the rise in interest rates in January 2022.

Gilt-edged bonds pay interest each year, again guaranteed but relatively low interest. Investment property will produce a rental income and will appreciate in value (in the good times but not so much at the moment in the pandemic), and the purchase of shares should, in the ideal world, produce a dividend and possibly capital growth, depending on the share. Again, like everything, the more solid investment, as we shall see, such as in companies characterised as 'Blue Chip' companies, will generally produce stable but lower returns.

An investor will usually consider the return on an asset as an annual percentage of its value. This is the rate of return, or the yield. The rate of return on a share is known as the dividend yield and is calculated in a similar way to interest from a bank or building society: the dividend paid by a company is divided by the price of the share as quoted on the stock market.

Dividend payments on shares are not guaranteed. Companies, for a variety of reasons, can decide not to pay a dividend. However, the other rate of return on shares, capital appreciation, is an equally important consideration to an investor.

Capital appreciation is the increase in value of any money invested. If inflation is higher than the rate of return then money will lose value. Shares are similar to other investments in this respect. They can fall in price as well as rise. Essentially, the total return on any asset comprises income received and the increase in value of that asset (capital growth).

Investors will need to look at the possibility of loss on assets. Different assets have different degrees of risk, usually relating to their potential for appreciation or depreciation. Deposits in banks will rarely if ever depreciate as periodic interest will be added and the investment will be protected apart from a possible loss of value due to inflation.

Ordinary shares carry risks of both falling prices and falling returns. A company's declining profits can result in a fall in the share price and also lead to a company deciding not to pay dividends. Many investors will usually try to create a portfolio of shares, ranging from more high-risk equities to safer homes, so that a fall in the value of one is offset by the growth in value of another. However, as we shall see in the summing up, discussion of investment strategies, it is better to limit the number of investments in order to retain control. *Basically, different assets have different degrees of return. The main principle is that the higher the return the higher the risk.*

Investors will also take into account the degree of ease with which they can convert their asset into cash if need arises. This is known as the liquidity of an asset. The liquidity of an asset will affect the return received. The more liquid an asset, as a general principle, the lower the return. Asset liquidity and asset values are also affected by time.

For example, the longer that money is tied up in a bank account the more illiquid that it is. Because of uncertainty about the future, money today is worth more than money tomorrow. To bring these values into balance, and to encourage saving and investing rather than spending, the longer that money is unavailable in the present, the greater the reward.

Hedging and speculation

When weighing up which assets to buy or to hold, an investor will keep coming back to the main consideration: risk. The more risk-averse investor will want as much protection of their assets value as possible. There are various means of achieving this. One basic strategy is called hedging, and it is a version of the strategy of portfolio diversification: the investor will hold two or more assets whose risk/return characteristics to some degree offset each other. One typical example is to hold one safe but low return asset for one high-risk one. A more precise way to hedge is to use derivatives, the range of securities whose price depends on or derives from the price of an underlying security. We will be discussing derivatives later in the book.

A put-option, for example, gives its owner the right, but not the obligation, to sell a share at a fixed price (the striking price) on or at a certain date. Owning a put -option with the share itself means that the investor's potential capital loss is limited to the loss implied should the share fall to the striking price. If it falls further the investor can use the option and sell at the striking price.

The speculator

On the other side of the hedgers trading is the speculator. This is someone who is prepared to take on the extra risk that the hedger wants to avoid. Speculators are in the market with the intention of making as much money as possible. They believe that they know the future prospects for asset prices better than the majority of investors, and hence are prepared to take bigger risks.

Investors, whether hedgers or speculators, who expect a rise in a particular asset price or in the market as a whole are known as **bulls,** whilst those who express pessimism about the future of the markets are known as **bears.**

Markets

Assets are bought and sold in markets. Markets are institutions that allow buyers and sellers to trade assets with one another through the discovery of prices with which both are satisfied. Some traders may meet in physical places. However, in the age of technology this is not necessary. Wherever and however the trading is carried out, what is actually happening is a form of auction. For example a trader may have 100 lots of assets to sell. If there are more or less traders at the suggested price (more or less than 100) the trader will lower or raise the price accordingly. This becomes the current market price.

Financial markets can be classified in different ways. One basic distinction is between primary and secondary markets. In primary markets, new money flows from lenders to borrowers as companies and governments seek new funds. In secondary markets investors buy and sell existing assets among themselves.

The existence of the secondary market is generally considered to be essential for a good primary market. The more liquid the secondary market, the easier it should be to raise capital in the primary market by persuading investors to take on new assets. The secondary market allows them to sell should they decide that it is an asset that they don't want to hold.

Markets may also be classified by whether or not they are organised and whether they are regulated by an institution. For example, the London Stock Exchange is an organised market while the over-the-counter derivatives market is not.

Markets can be classified by the nature of the assets traded on them: stocks, bonds, derivatives, currencies, commodities and so on. All of these are distinct markets and there are strong connections between them. These connections grow stronger as increasing globalisation and improved technology allows better flows of information. An investor will need this diverse but interlinked information to allow them to compare and contrast different investments.

****

Ch. 2

The Benefits of Owning Stocks and Shares

In chapter one, we looked briefly at the aims of the individual investor and how they might spend their money. When looking at shares as opposed to other savings and investments, it has to be said that the number of ways a person can invest amounts of their hard earned cash is limited.

Because most people need access to their capital to fund a whole range of short and longer term projects, such as holidays, education and so on, buying shares usually ranks way down the list as an investment.

Shares are usually a longer-term investment and the risk involved in the investment depends on the timescale of that investment. Rewards can be measured more easily if a longer term has been allowed to elapse. The stock market provides a fairly good home for investments for those people who are prepared to accept a degree of risk and can wait for the right moment before cashing in and pulling out. Essentially, money invested in the stock market should not be money that you need to realize at short notice or money that will be realized for your old age. The stock market is only for people who have spare cash to invest and can weather the storm if a loss is made. It is not for those who will lay awake at night worrying about losing money on shares.

If you do decide to invest in the stock market, and there are about 12 million people who have done so in the U.K, then don't put everything you have to invest in the market at once. Keep some aside to invest when a really good opportunity arises. There are two ways to invest in the stock market, long term (suitable for the small investor) and as an active trader.

Long-term investment

It is true to say that in the long term the stock market has produced a better return on investment than any other alternative form of investment. All of the charts produced to indicate growth have demonstrated that over a period of 30, 50 and more years, returns from shares outperform most other investments. Shares in Britain have, since 1918, produced a return of over 12% a year compared with other investments such as government issued gilt edged securities which have produced just over 6%.

This return on shares has been in the face of the periodic cyclical downturns in the economy and in overseas economies. Cash in a deposit account would have produced 5% in the same period. However, cash in a deposit account is safe and as we have seen shares can be a risk.

When considering the long term, questions of future economic stability will always arise. For sure, at different periods economies will fluctuate (the current pandemic induced recession being the worst since the 1930's) and losses will occur but in the longer term these tend to even out and share prices rise, as history has demonstrated.

It is up to the investor to decide what they want from an investment. Do you want income or capital growth? These are not absolute alternatives, since companies that do well hand out handsome dividends (usually) and see their share price rise. Unit trusts and investment trusts as we have seen provide good homes for savings and, at the very least will ensure inflationary growth.

Short-term investments

As discussed above, this is another way of investing, but it is for the experts and people who are sufficiently clued up and will devote time to study the markets. This is the short-term active trading that is built on the tactic of taking advantage whenever share prices move sharply enough to make trading beneficial. The active short-term trader will watch the markets very carefully and look for opportunities such as takeovers and mergers where they can buy and sell relatively quickly at a profit.

Short-term investing usually requires more money than longer term investing as the costs of trading can be higher as brokers fees and government taxes have to be paid.

Perks of owning shares

In addition to the usual benefits of owning shares, such as appreciation of capital and dividend income, many companies try to keep shareholders loyal by offering perks, usually in the form of discounts of one form or another. Channel tunnel has travel concessions offered to shareholders, other nationally known companies such as Iceland and Kwik Fit all provide benefits to investors. A number of fund managers will provide a list of companies that provide perks for shareholders.

****

SECTION 2

OPERATIONS OF THE STOCK MARKET AND THE NATURE OF COMPANIES

Ch.3

The Stock Market and How it Works-Share Trading

What is a Stock Exchange?

A stock exchange is a marketplace that enables the buying and selling of shares in publicly listed companies. Whilst the concept of what a stock exchange is has remained consistent throughout history, how they operate has evolved considerably over time. In this post we explain what the London Stock Exchange is and how it has evolved into the Exchange we know today.

The history of the London Stock Exchange

Its origins can be traced back to the 17th century. Stock brokers would gather in London coffee houses to buy and sell shares.

The London Stock Exchange was formally established in 1801 and began enlisting members. The Exchange provided physical facilities across the UK for members to buy and sell shares.

Following a period of growth throughout the 20th century operations were centralised in London with the establishment of the Stock Exchange Tower in 1972.

In 1986 deregulation of the UK stock market opened up huge possibilities for new investors to access the market and become shareholders. It also saw a move away from open out-cry trading. This was where traders would shout and use hand signals to carry out trades. Instead, the use of technology was introduced. The deregulation is often called the "big bang" of the stock market.

The modern-day

Today, its headquarters are in Paternoster Square, having re-located there in 2004.

The London Stock Exchange Group, the company that manages the Exchange was formed in 2007 following a merger between the London Stock Exchange and the Milan Stock Exchange (Borsa Italiana). The group state they employ 4500 people globally.

Nearly all trading is carried out electronically now, in contrast to the days of the past. The Exchange hosts and manages the technology that allows this to happen.

How big is the Exchange?

The London Stock Exchange is one of largest in the world. The Exchange is home to over 2000 companies with a total market value of approximately £4 trillion. The market value for each company is calculated by multiplying the share price by the number of shares issued.

According to London Stock Exchange Group data, 272.6 million trades were made in 2018 at an eye-watering total trade value of £1.4 trillion. That equates to an average of 750,000 trades per day.

The primary markets traded on the London Stock Exchange

There are two primary markets that provide access to shares of the 2000+ companies listed on the Stock Exchange.

Main Market

There are approximately 1200 companies listed on the Main Market with a total share value of £3.9 trillion (as at 2020). The Main Market contains the larger companies including those part of the FTSE index.

What's the difference between the different FTSE's?

Within the London Stock Exchange there are various indexes (essentially categories), the make-up of which is determined by the total market value of a company's shares. These indexes are called the FTSE (Financial Times Stock Exchange) indexes. The indexes are managed by FTSE Russell who are a subsidiary of the London Stock Exchange Group.

The different FTSE indexes on the Main Market are:

- **FTSE 100** — the largest 100 companies. Here you will find some extremely well known names.
- **FTSE 250** — the next tier down, so the 101st to the 350th largest companies.
- **FTSE 350** – a combination of the FTSE 100 and FTSE 250 companies.

- **FTSE SmallCap** — the companies that meet the FTSE criteria but are too small to quality for the top 350.
- **FTSE All Share**— all the companies in the FTSE 100, FTSE 250 and FTSE Small Cap indexes.
- **FTSE Fledgling** – companies who are listed on the Main Market but are not large enough to qualify for the other indexes.

How the London Stock Exchange works

The Stock Exchange provides a mechanism for companies to raise capital to fund their business. The process of a company listing their shares on the exchange for the first time is often called an Initial Public Offer (IPO) or Floating.

The London Stock Exchange allows companies from around the world to list, not just UK companies. Actually, over 50 countries are represented in total. The exchange provides a mechanism for people around the world to trade shares in the companies listed on it. In addition, the Stock Exchange provides information such as share prices and regulatory news. There are certain announcements that companies listed on the stock market are obliged to publish. These include details of trades in the company made by directors, changes to positions of the board of directors and financial updates.

It is worth mentioning that the Exchange also allows investors to trade more complex financial products beyond shares.

A simple explanation

The London Stock Exchange provides a facility for companies to issue shares to raise funds for their business. The Stock Exchange acts as a marketplace for investors to buy and sell the shares the companies have issued.

Listing a business on the LSE Main Market

There are several steps a company needs to consider when listing a business on the London Stock Exchange Main Market.

Appointing advisers

In order to join the London Stock Exchange Main Market, a company must have certain advisers in place. They may already have advisers who have the relevant public market experience, or they may need to seek recommendations to appoint new ones. Each adviser plays a vital role in the application and admission process for the Main Market:

A sponsor or corporate adviser - for a Premium Listing on the Main Market, a company must appoint and use a sponsor to guide the company through the application and admission process, and to advise on the UK Listing Authority's (UKLA's) legal requirements. For companies on a Standard Listing, a corporate adviser may be appointed instead.

A broker - a broker will assist with the pricing of the companies shares and help generate interest in their business by marketing it when the company is admitted to trading and thereafter.

A reporting accountant - an accountant will independently review the company's financial position and produce a number of reports to meet specific regulatory requirements and to assist the directors or the sponsor in meeting their obligations.

A lawyer - a lawyer will be able to advise the company on any legal issues that might arise as a result of admission to the Main Market, including the necessary disclosure requirements and continuing obligations.

Preparing a company for the Main Market

It is necessary to review the following aspects of a company before beginning the listing process:

Assets and liabilities – it is necessary to ensure that the company owns or controls all of the assets needed for the operation of the company and that they can cover any liabilities

Shareholder arrangements – it is necessary to ensure that any current shareholders agree a time-limit restriction on selling their shares after flotation

Share capital – it is necessary to organise how to split the new share capital, or re-organise the current capital the company has

Contracts - formalise any important contracts – e.g. for personnel, suppliers, sub-contractors, etc

Intellectual property (IP) - ensure that any valuable IP is protected before flotation

Insurance - ensure that all insurance policies are up to date and provide adequate cover

Joining the Main Market

The length of time it will take to join the Main Market will depend on a number of factors, including the chosen route to market and on the company's fundraising requirements. Once they have appointed advisers they should be able to agree a realistic timescale for joining the Main Market. Once they have appointed advisers, they must also:

Create a prospectus – the company must produce a prospectus which will be verified by the UKLA. This will also be the main marketing document and should contain enough information for investors to decide whether the business is a viable investment opportunity.

Apply for admission to trade – the company must apply to both London Stock Exchange and the UKLA to admit their securities to the Main Market. The applications will run simultaneously and the company must meet all the requirements of both organisations.

Market the flotation – the company should promote the flotation amongst potential investors to ensure success on admission day.

Complete the underwriting agreement – the company should enter into a placing or underwriting agreement between relevant parties such as brokers, directors and selling shareholders.

Hold an impact day - the impact day is when the prospectus is approved and published, and flotation is announced.

Once a company has successfully completed these tasks, the company's shares will be admitted to trading on the Main Market, and trading can commence.

Other UK markets-The Alternative Investment Market (AIM)

The Alternative Investment Market (AIM) is a sub-market of the London Stock Exchange (LSE) that is designed to help smaller companies access capital from the public market.

AIM allows these companies to raise capital by listing on a public exchange with much greater regulatory flexibility compared to the main market.

The companies listed on AIM tend to be small-cap and more highly speculative companies in nature, in part due to AIM's relaxed regulations and listing requirements. The AIM unit was launched in 1995 and now is host to more than 3,500 corporate share listings.

Understanding the Alternative Investment Market (AIM)

The FTSE Group maintains three indexes for tracking the AIM: the FTSE AIM UK 50 Index, the FTSE AIM 100 Index and the FTSE AIM All-Share Index.

Companies seeking to do an initial public offering (IPO) and list on AIM are usually small companies that have exhausted their access to private capital but are not at the level required to undergo an IPO and list on a large exchange. Although AIM is still referred to as the Alternative Investment Market, or London's

Alternative Investment Market in the financial press, the LSE has made a practice of referring to it by its acronym only.

AIM and the Nomads

The process for a company listing on AIM follows much the same path as a traditional IPO, just with less stringent requirements. There is still a pre-IPO marketing blitz, with historical financial information to stir up interest, and a post-IPO lock up, for example. One key difference is the role nominee advisors, commonly known as nomads, play in the process. These nomads are seen as the regulatory system for AIM and are tasked with advising the companies pre-IPO and carrying out the due diligence that investors expect to vet the prospectus. One issue that is frequently raised about this relationship is the fact that nomads are responsible for ensuring regulatory compliance, but they also profit in the form of fees from the companies they list and continue to oversee as part of the listing agreement.

AIM's Reputation as an Unregulated Market

AIM is seen as a more speculative investment forum due to its relaxed regulations compared to larger exchanges. The regulation for companies listed on AIM is often referred to as being light touch regulation, as it is essentially a self-regulated market where nomads are tasked with adhering to the broad guidelines.

There have been cases of nomads failing to do their duties, as it were, and AIM is not a stranger to outright fraud (to be fair, no major exchange is either). As a result, AIM tends to attract sophisticated and institutional investors who have the risk appetite and resource to perform independent due diligence. AIM has been criticized for being a financial wild west where companies with questionable ethics go for money. This criticism has held up in some cases, particularly with extraction companies operating in impoverished regions of the world. However, AIM has also shown the value of having a gap market where risk-hungry investors can help accelerate cash-starved companies along their growth path, benefiting the company, its investors and the economy as a whole.

TechMark

TechMARK and techMARK mediscience are specially developed segments of the London Stock Exchange's Main Market, designed for companies at the forefront of innovative technology.

TechMARK was launched in November 1999 by the Exchange to create new opportunities for companies whose business is dependent on technological innovation, and for investors in those companies. Two years later, techMARK mediscience was then launched to focus on companies whose business is dependent on innovation in the development or manufacture of pharmaceuticals, or products or services that are wholly or substantially dedicated to the healthcare industry.

TechMARK brings together companies whose business models require a particularly high level of innovation and investment into research and development programmes. By providing a spotlight on this segment of the Main Market, it helps techMARK companies to build successful relationships with investors – vital to innovation and funding discovery. And for scientific-research based companies, the Listing Rules take into account business specialisation and facilitate admission to the Main Market.

Who can join?

TechMARK is open to all innovative companies, regardless of size, sector or commercial or industrial activity, country of origin or currency of share trading. There is a broad range of companies operating in numerous sectors on techMARK, from software and computer services to oil and gas and even transport.

TechMARK mediscience companies operate within the techMARK family. TechMARK mediscience specifically includes healthcare sectors such as medical equipment, medical supplies, biotechnology and pharmaceuticals. All techMARK companies share one key attribute – commitment to innovation, research and development.

Ofex

Ofex (Off Exchange) is the UK's independent public market, dedicated to smaller companies, and based on a quote-driven trading platform. It was owned and operated by PLUS Markets Group plc, which was acquired by ICAP in 2012 and rebranded as

ICAP Securities and Derivatives Exchange (ISDX). It is authorised and regulated by the Financial Services Authority. The Market Abuse regime covers all securities traded on the Ofex market.

Since launch, Ofex has served over 500 companies and has not only provided a market for those companies' shares, but also an opportunity to raise equity-based finance. It is a flexible market, with broad appeal to companies, their professional investors, and those investors wishing to invest in smaller companies. Its robust regulatory framework strikes a careful balance between flexibility for smaller company management teams and the protection required by equity capital investors. A competing market-maker system supports buying and selling shares in Ofex companies, offering liquidity and independent valuation. Investors in UK-based Ofex companies enjoy the tax benefits associated with holding investments in unquoted securities. Information about the Ofex market can be found at www. isdx.com

SWX Europe (formerly Virt X)

This incorporates a small rival to the London Stock Exchange called Tradepoint, which started as an electronic order book in 1995 and was itself quoted on AIM. In combination with the Swiss Stock Exchange SWX, it created Virt X (now SWX Europe), with offices in London and Zurich although all trading is carried out from Zurich. In addition to trading in the normal UK quoted stocks, it has set up clearance and registry systems to allow trading in Eurotop, which shows the largest companies in Europe.

The IPSX

The International Property Securities Exchange operates the world's first regulated stock exchange dedicated to commercial property providing a public stock market solely for the admission and trading of shares in companies owning and managing commercial property assets. IPSX provides asset owners, both investors and owner occupiers, the ability to partially release capital value in a single asset whilst retaining the ability to have control. IPSX provides investors access to the commercial property asset class by providing a proxy to direct ownership. IPSX allows investors to buy and sell shares in listed single asset commercial property companies providing yield in a tax efficient security. The Financial Conduct Authority has issued a Recognition Order in respect of IPSX UK Limited and is designated as a Recognised Investment Exchange. IPSX has joined a small group of securities exchanges in the UK – all of which are operated by major international market infrastructure groups. The Exchange operates an "EU Regulated Market", which provides asset owners with the potential to access the widest pool of institutional and private investors. For more information visit ipsx.com

****

Ch. 4.

General Points about Trading on the Stock Markets

What does the existence of these multiple trading markets mean to the small investor? It means two things. It means that you have easier access to trade shares of companies beyond those that are listed and traded on the London Stock Exchange.

A customers order can be routed to any FSA authorised market where the security trades. Each brokerage firm decides where to route the buy and sell orders it handles.

A brokerage firm tries to get the best price for its customer. This means executing an order to buy securities (stocks, bonds, ETF's (exchange traded funds-more later) etc at the lowest price available at the time the order reached the trading market. When a customer places an order to sell, the brokerage firm tries to execute the order at the highest price available.

The basic order types

It is important to understand the meaning of the different types of buy and sell orders used by brokers to get a trade executed in a specific way. Basically, unless you have an idea of what stock brokers are talking about you will find yourself at a disadvantage.

A typical small investor will find that five basic order types will serve most of their investment needs:

- A market order
- A limit order
- A marketable limit order
- A stop order
- A stop-limit order

It is important to understand how each order works and the possible result associated with using each. One basic feature of orders must be clearly understood first. When an order ticket is marked it can be marked in one of four ways:

BUY

'BUY' means the investor is acquiring a securities position with the expectation that the price will rise over time. The words' Buy' and 'Long' are synonyms in the investment market.

SELL LONG

Order tickets are not simply marked 'sell'. Each ticket must specify whether it is an order to 'sell long' or 'sell short'. Sell long means an investor is selling securities that they already own.

SELL SHORT

'Sell short' is more complicated. It means that the investor is selling securities that he or she does not own. In fact, the securities that are being sold short have been borrowed on the investors behalf by the brokerage firm. The investor is expecting the market price of the securities to decline over the short term so they can buy them back at a lower price. The difference between the higher price at which the securities are initially sold short and the lower price at which they are eventually bought back is the profit to the investor. Needless to say, for the small investor this is a route that is better left alone.

BUY TO COVER

'Buy to cover' means the investor is liquidating a short position. In reality, when the brokerage firm gets this order it buys back the securities that were sold short for the investor. Remember, the brokerage firm had borrowed the securities for the customer. Now it returns these to the lender, which is usually another brokerage firm.

The five basic order types
A market order

A market order, whether placed with a broker or using an electronic order ticket, contains only the name of the security and the amount in pounds. It does not specify a price or time, as the examples below illustrate:

buy £1,000 of BT

-or-

Sell £1,000 of Vodafone

A market order must be executed immediately at the BBO, best bid price or offer price, available in the market at that time.

Limit Order

When placing a limit order, the investor specifies the price at which he or she wants to buy a specific security. For example: Sell £1,000 of Shell at 1.39p

-or- Buy £1,000 of Mears Group at 500p

Importantly, when a limit order is placed, it is understood that the order will be executed only at the specified price or better. the investor who wants to sell wants 1.39p or better. Those who want to sell or want to buy want a certain price or lower.

Marketable limit order

This is a variation on the limit order that is used on many of the computerised order-matching systems. Unlike a traditional limit order, which is entered below or above the market, a marketable limit order is entered at the current price level at which a share is trading. In placing this order, a customer is making sure that the order will be executed only at the current price level or better.

If, for example, a share is trading at 660p and you want to buy shares at this price only, you would enter a marketable limit order with a specified price of 660p. Your order would be eligible for immediate execution. The advantage of a marketable limit order is that if the share price unexpectedly moved above 660p, then your order would not be executed. If the share price moved lower then your order would be executed because the lower price is better than the specified price.

Stop order

Like a limit order, an investor must specify a price, called the stop price, when the order is placed. However, with a stop order, when the security's price hits the specified price, the order is transformed into a market order, and is executed at the security's current BBO, whatever that may be. This is the most useful order for investors who want to limit losses and protect profits. The example below illustrates this.

Let's say that you have just bought a company's shares, which are trading at 660p. When you buy these shares you are, of course, concerned that the price might decline suddenly, resulting in a significant loss. To limit your potential loss you place a sell stop order at 640p, below the price at which you bought the stock. It is important to understand that the price that you specify on a sell stop order is only a trigger. If the share price suddenly plummets and hits your 640p price, the order is immediately transformed into a market order. Subsequently, it is executed at whatever the market price might be at the moment, which may be above or below the stop price. In this case, the sell stop order would limit your loss on the position to around 20p. The loss could be greater if the share price is in free fall

Stop limit order

When an investor places a stop limit order, he or she must specify a stop price and a limit price. For example:

Sell £1,000 of Costain at 3.20p stop 3.50 limit

-or- But £1,000 of Mears at 500p 520 limit

On a sell stop limit order, the limit price is the same or lower than the stop price and on a buy stop limit order the limit price will be the same or higher than the stop price. Although some of the above may sound a little confusing, especially for the first time investor, it is worthwhile knowing the basics of share sale or purchase terminology.

There are numerous websites that will provide more information on the types of stock ordering, such www.thebalance.com.

****

Ch. 5

Companies, and Financial Data-Interpreting Data

Companies are organisations established for some kind of commerce and with a legal identity separate from their owners. The owners are the shareholders who have the right to part of a company's profit, and who usually have limited liability. This means that their liability is limited to the value of the shares that they own.

Companies are often run by people other than the owners, although in theory it is the ordinary shareholders who control the company. However, the ordinary shareholders will be the last in the queue of claimants should a company go under. Companies can be classified as limited liability or public limited companies.

It is with the latter that we will be concerned here as PLC's, as they are known, are listed on the stock exchange and their shares are traded on the market, such as the UK Stock Market, which we will discuss in the next chapter.

Company data

The primary source for any data and for analysis of a company is its annual report and accounts. These documents will provide all the information on a company's business and financial affairs and its obligations to its shareholders. We will be looking at interpretation of company accounts later in the book.

The annual report and accounts will describe the current trading conditions of the company, what it has sold (its turnover, sales and revenues) and what it has paid out in wages or salaries, rent, raw materials and any other inputs to the costs of production. The documents will also indicate the profit or loss position, the state of assets and liabilities at the start and end of the financial year and the cash flow situation.

Profit and loss

A company's profit and loss account is a statement of the final outcome of all its transactions, all revenues and costs during a given period, usually a year. It shows whether the company made any money in the previous year, how it made the money and how it spends the profits. Comparisons will also be made with previous years and also with other company's performance.

The total value of all goods sold by the company is known as its sales or turnover. Deducting from the turnover the costs of producing goods will give you an operating profit figure. Deducting from that figure, in turn, the costs of interest payments to banks and other parties, will give you a pre-tax profit. It is this profit that is reported in the financial pages.

The next deduction is tax. Corporation tax is paid by the company on profits after all costs have been met except for dividends paid out to ordinary shareholders. Advance corporation tax, which is income tax paid on behalf of ordinary shareholders and their dividend income, is also payable.

Money left once taxation demands have been met is known as after-tax profit or equity earnings. This is now at the disposal of the company for distribution as dividends or reinvestment in the business.

The balance sheet

The balance sheet is a snapshot of a company's capital position at an instant in time and details everything it owns (assets) against everything it owes (liabilities) at year-end. The two sides of a balance sheet, by definition, should balance. Essentially, liabilities are monies borrowed to invest in assets.

A companies assets are made up of two items: fixed or long-term assets, such as building and equipment, current and short term assets, such as stocks of goods for sale, debtors or accounts receivable and cash in the bank. Its liabilities are made up of three items, the first being current or short term liabilities, such as trade credit or accounts payable, tax, dividends and overdrafts at the bank and longer-term debt such as loans and mortgages etc.

The third form of liability is that of ordinary funds and this in turn divides into three forms: revenue reserves or retained earnings-the company's trading profits that have not been distributed as dividends; capital reserves-surpluses from sources other than normal trading such as revaluation of fixed assets or gains due to advantageous currency fluctuations; and issued ordinary shares. Ordinary shares have three different values; their nominal value, the face, or par, value at which they were issued and their book value which is the total of ordinary funds divided by the number of shares in issue; and their market value, the price quoted on the stock exchange.

Cash flow statements

The cash flow statement details the amount of money that flows in and out of a company in a given period of time. The cash flow statement will track flows of money.

The balance sheet is a check of a company's financial health, and the profit and loss account is an indicator of its current success or failure. Together they can be used to calculate a number of valuable ratios.

Interpretation of company accounts

Having taken a cursory look at company accounts, looking at profit and loss, the balance sheet and cash-flow information it is now time to dig deeper and look at key ratios that highlight a company's position and allow the would be shareholder to take investment decisions.

It is tempting just to read financial pages and make a decision about the health of a company from information contained therein. However, if you want to make a serious attempt at investing in shares then you need to be in a position to make your own analysis. There are a number of key indicators from which you can measure a company's performance. They are all contained within the annual report. There are several crucial indicators, which in addition to being in the accounts are published in papers such as the financial times each day. These are dividend yield and the price earnings ratio and also dividend cover. For the small private investor the most useable of the key indicators are the return on capital employed, gearing, income gearing and pre-tax profit margin. Using the three mentioned above together with these four the private investor will be able to judge whether or not the company is a sound investment.

Key financial ratios

The four financial ratios, return on capital employed, gearing, income gearing and pre-tax profit margin are reasonably easy to work out. In annual reports they will be over a two-year period so that changes over time are reflected. Often, a report will include a section on 'facts for shareholders' or a five year record which include some calculated ratios. However, quite often these ratios are calculated in certain ways and it is always better to carry out your own calculation. Below is an indication of the basic calculation of the key ratios.

Gearing

Gearing compares the amount of money in shareholders funds with the amount of external liabilities that the company has. High gearing is more risky than low gearing as it means that a higher level of external liability exists. This, of course could be for many reasons, such as company expansion and so on. There are a number of ways of calculating gearing but one of the main ways also effectively highlights a company's exposure and vulnerability. The ratio is a comparison between the total debt liabilities of a company and its shareholders funds. The more the debt and the higher the interest payments the lower the profits and the lower potential for paying out dividends of any worth. To make the calculation: find current liabilities in the annual report, often called 'liabilities: amounts falling due within one year'. Add 'creditors: amounts falling due after more than one year' ensuring that everything is included, to find total debt liabilities. Next, find the figure for total shareholders funds, but do not include minority interests. Divide total debt liabilities by total shareholders funds and multiply by 100 to arrive at a percentage figure.

The rule of thumb is as follows:

Low gearing = below 100%
Medium gearing = 100-200%
High gearing = above 200%

Income gearing

This ratio demonstrates a company's ability to service its debt. Income gearing will reveal this information. It is the ratio of interest payable to the profits out of which that interest must be paid. Obviously, all companies wish to keep interest payments as low as possible.

A lot of investors regard income gearing as the most important ratio. To calculate income gearing: find the interest payable for the year, which is often expressed as a detail in the notes. The figure on the balance sheet is 'net interest' which is interest payable minus interest receivable. Find the earnings, or profit, before interest and tax. Often this must be calculated by adding interest payable to the pre-tax profit shown on the profit and loss account. Divide interest payable by profit before interest and tax and multiply by 100 to express it as a percentage. The outcome can be read as follows:

Low income gearing = below 25%

Medium income gearing = 26-75%

High income gearing = above 75%

Return on capital employed

This measure is an indicator of how efficiently management is performing. It relates pre-tax profit to the level of long-term capital invested in the business. It is a good guide as to whether enough return is being generated to maintain and grow dividends and avoid future cash flow problems.

To calculate ROCE: capital employed is equivalent to total assets minus current liabilities and this figure is usually demonstrated on the balance sheet. If it isn't then it should be calculated as long-term debt, plus provisions for liabilities and charges, plus any other long term liabilities, plus shareholders funds, plus minority interests. Divide pre-tax profit by capital employed and multiply it by 100 to express it as a percentage. The calculation should be interpreted as follows:

Low profitability = below 10%

Medium profitability = 10-20%

High profitability = above 20%

Pre-tax profit margin

This ratio will reveal the profits earned per pound of sales and therefore measures the efficiency of the operation. It is an indicator of the company's ability to withstand adverse trading conditions such as falling prices, rising costs or declining sales. To calculate the pre-tax profit margin: take the pre-tax profit figure on the profit and loss account. Divide it by the total sales revenues (sales turnover) and multiply it for a percentage. The calculation can be interpreted as such:

Low margin = below 2%

Medium margin = 2-8%

High margin = above 8%

The above is a basic guide that will enable you to read and interpret a company's accounts and to gain a clearer idea whether or not to invest or steer clear.

It is now time to take a look at the various avenues that a company will take to raise finance and also a description of some of the terms that you may come across on a daily basis, but not fully understand.

Ch. 6

Companies Raising Finance

From the perspective of a company, the financial markets exist to raise money through various financial instruments. There are basically three sources of capital: permanent capital of shareholders (also known as equity capital), ordinary shares or in the USA, common stock; ploughed back profits (equity funds or shareholders reserves): various forms of debt or loan capital. Corporate finance will usually focus on the relative benefits of financing via debt or equity.

Equity

Equity finance is the capital that allows companies to take the risks inherent in embarking on new business projects. This equity finance is derived from shareholders. There are two common classes of equity capital: *ordinary shares*, (see below) which have no guaranteed amount of dividend payment, but which carry voting rights; and *preference shares*, (see below) which usually carry a fixed dividend and have preference over ordinary shareholders if the company is wound-up but carry no voting rights. There are basic variations on these which are discussed throughout the book.

Ordinary shares

Ordinary shares are the shares most frequently issued when a company does a floatation or initial public offering. Ordinary shares are part of every PLC's or limited company's capital structure.

The total number of shares that a company is authorised to issue is specified in its Articles of Association. Investors who own a company's ordinary shares have rights that are stated in the company's Articles of association. These rights are:

Right to vote

Ordinary shares are sometimes called voting shares because only they offer owners this right, preference shares, discussed below, do not. Among the important issues ordinary shareholders can vote on are:

- Election of board of directors
- Changes in the Articles of Association
- A merger, acquisition or occasionally a major disposal
- An increase in the authorised capital
- Directors Remuneration.

Voting takes place at the Annual General Meeting and at an Extraordinary General Meeting (EGM) if one is held. If shareholders attend either of these meetings they can ask questions and vote themselves. If they choose not to attend they can sign a proxy giving someone else the right to vote on their behalf (usually a board member or large shareholder). In the UK, companies issue one class of ordinary shares, whilst in the US the company will issue two, one to company insiders and one to members of the public.

Right to receive dividends

All dividends must be declared by a company's board of directors and are usually paid out twice a year, although some companies pay quarterly.

The amount of payment is totally at the boards discretion. Generally, it is thought that a company will pay dividends according to its profitability. However, since the onset of the recession, some companies choose to withhold dividends which has resulted in investors withdrawing shares and looking for other companies to invest in.

Some boards believe in paying regular and substantial dividends and increase payments regularly. They do this to send a signal to shareholders that the company is reliable and a good investment. The shareholders of these companies are usually people who rely on an income on which to live. Pharmaceutical companies are good examples of this type of company.

An example of the opposite type of company is Berkshire Hathaway, Warren Buffet's investment vehicle. He doesn't believe in paying regular dividends but encourages investors to buy and hold onto their shares for the longer term.

In the past, companies gave shareholders the right to receive additional ordinary shares in the company instead of a cash dividend payment. This is known as a *scrip offering.* However, fewer and fewer companies in the UK now offer this alternative.

Pre-emptive rights

This is the right of each ordinary shareholder to maintain his or her proportionate ownership in the company. If, for example, you own 10% of a company's issued and outstanding shares and the company proposes issuing an additional 1,000,000 new shares, then you, the ordinary shareholder, have the right of first refusal to buy 10% of the new shares. This right is implemented through a *rights issue.* Existing shareholders have the right to subscribe to their percentage of the new offering within a limited period of time, usually 30 or 60 days. During this period, existing shareholders can purchase their portion of the new shares at a subscription price, which is usually lower than the share's current market price.

The shareholder has a second option. he or she can sell the rights to someone who really wants to subscribe to the additional shares. The shareholder's third option is to simply let the rights expire at the end of the designated period. If the shareholder decides on this route then the company can sell the shares to new investors.

Claims on a company's assets in liquidation

An ordinary shareholder has claims on a company's remaining assets should it go into liquidation. However, ordinary shareholders are last in line behind all other types of securities issued by a company. Losing all of the money that you have invested in a company is the biggest risk that a shareholder faces.

Classification of ordinary shares

Ordinary shares are frequently categorised according to where the company is in its development or growth. These classifications include:

- **Blue chip shares**. These are shares of large, usually multinational companies that have maintained market share as well as profits and earnings growth over many years and through various economic conditions. Blue chip stocks tend to pay steady dividends and increase the amount periodically.
- **Income stock.** These are companies that reliably pay a high percentage of their earnings as dividends. They usually operate in mature industries where turnover is relatively consistent and growth steady. Utility companies generally fall into this category.
- **Growth stocks.** Shares referred to as growth stocks are frequently in new business areas that are expanding rapidly. These companies typically pay little or no dividend. Instead, the company reinvests its earnings into research and development and investors will need to be in for the longer term. The capital growth of the share might increase year on year as the company grows.

- **Penny stock.** These shares are valued at less than £1, and are cheap, highly speculative shares of small, emerging businesses, or shares of once high-flying companies. Investors realise that the share price is so low that it can only go up.

Preference shares

This type of security is seldom issued in the UK today and only a few are still listed on the London Stock Exchange. Preference shares give holders similar rights over a company's shares as ordinary shares. However, usually, holders do not have rights to vote at company meetings. Like bonds they get specified payments at fixed future dates.

The term 'preference share', signifies their privileged status, since holders of preference shares are entitled to a dividend whether the company is making a profit or not. This obviously will make them attractive to investors who want a fixed income. If the company is not in a position to pay a dividend on a preference share with cumulative entitlements, then the dividend will be 'rolled up' and paid in full when the company is able.

Preference shareholders rank higher than ordinary shareholders when it comes to dividends. They rank behind debenture holders and creditors for liquidations and dividends. There are combinations of various classes of preference shares that will be set out when the shares are purchased.

Dilution of equity and alternative borrowings

An increase in the number of ordinary shares in a company without a corresponding increase in its assets or profitability results in a decrease in the value of the shares. This is known as dilution of equity.

To avoid immediate dilution of the shares in issue, a company might use an alternative financial instrument to raise capital, a convertible (also known as a convertible loan stock or a convertible bond). These are debt instruments that can be converted into ordinary or preference shares at a fixed date and price in the future. Their value to a company, besides avoiding dilution, is that in exchange for their potential conversion value, they will carry a lower rate of interest than standard debt.

(**Redeemable** shares come with an agreement that the company can buy them back at a future date - this can be at a fixed date or at the choice of the business. A company cannot issue only redeemable shares).

Other types of borrowings

Businesses issue a variety of 'paper' which are used to raise capital. In addition to raising capital from shareholders, a company may need to borrow in the short term and longer-term and may issue bonds or other forms of paper. For borrowings a company may issue what is in effect a corporate I.O.U. This will come in the form of a bond. Bonds can be traded, are long term with an undertaking to pay regular interest, at a rate fixed at time of issue (normally) and with a specified date at which they must be redeemed. Some of these bonds are backed by assets of the company and some are unsecured. Like all loans, the interest rate will reflect the status of the bond.

Loan stocks and debentures

Bonds that have no security are called loan stocks or notes. Debentures are underwritten by assets. These types of paper are different from shares in that, notwithstanding the performance of the company, they must be repaid at the specified time. Shares, as we have seen, do not. As the rate of interest on bonds and debentures is fixed the market price of the paper will go up as interest rates go down and vice-versa. This factor underpins the attractiveness or otherwise of bonds as an investment. Because the rate is fixed at issue the investor knows how much the return will be, assuming the company stays solvent, right up to the date of redemption.

Any investor in bonds will need to look at the company as a whole and its future prospects of staying afloat before investing.

If an issuer defaults on repayments, usually because of going bankrupt, debenture holders can appoint their own receiver to realise the assets which act as their security and repay them the capital. Unsecured loan stockholders do not have this option but will still rank ahead of shareholders in repayment. There are different types of debentures which will take preference over each other depending on the nature of the paper, i.e.

subordinated debentures will have less preference than an un-subordinated debenture.

Warrants

Warrants give the owner the right to buy ordinary shares (equities) usually over a specified period at a predetermined rate, which is known as the strike, or exercise, price. Warrants have a definable value and are traded on the stock market, with the price directly related to the underlying shares. The value is the then market value of the share minus the strike price. For example, if the share currently stands at £2 and the cost of converting the warrant into ordinary shares has been set at £1.50 then the price of the warrant would be 50p. If the shares then increase to £5 then the price of the warrant would be £3.

Convertibles

Certain types of preference shares and corporate bonds are convertible. This basically means that during their lives the holders receive a regular dividend income but there is also a fixed date when the issues can be transformed into ordinary shares. This conversion is at the owner's choice, not the issuers.

Gilts

Gilt is short for gilt-edged securities. These bonds are held to be safe and dependable. They are not issued by companies but they are issued by the British government and, by virtue of being backed by the country as an asset, the risk is seen as zero.

Gilts are issued because politicians mortgage the future of the country. For example, when tax revenues are suffering, because of a dip in the economy, government bonds will be issued. They have a fixed rate of interest and are redeemable at a specified time in the future. There are normally a range of specified dates to ensure more flexibility for the government. The interest rate at issue is determined by the prevailing interest rate and also the target audience, who the specific issue is aimed at. Most gilts on issue are of this type.

There are index-linked gilts and also irredeemable bonds, such as the notorious War Loan, issued to people who backed the national effort during World War Two. Unfortunately, people who backed the war effort ended up with virtually nothing as inflation after the war eroded their value.

The list of gilts being traded along with dates of redemption is extensive. There are shorts (lives of under 5 years), medium dated (between 5-15 years) and longs with over 15 years to redemption. Most quality newspapers carry lists of these bonds and rates of interest. These papers will have the 'yield' rate, one being called the running yield, which is the return you would get at that quoted price and the redemption yield which calculates the stream of interest payments and also the value of holding them to redemption and getting them repaid-always at £100 par, the face value of the security.

Since the return on the bonds is fixed at issue, when the price of gilts goes up the yield goes down. Therefore, if you buy a gilt with nominal face value of 100p (£1) and with an interest rate set at issue of 10%, but the current price of that issue is 120p, you would get a yield of 8.3% (10p as a percentage of 120p). If the price of that issue falls to 80p you could get a yield of 12.5% (10p as a percentage of 80p).

There are, in addition to gilts, other public bonds issued by the government at a slightly higher risk. These include bonds issued by local authorities in a bid to raise money, and also overseas governments. The risk is very slight indeed. It is not likely that a local authority would renege on its bonds. Obviously, if you invest in a bond in a country which then undergoes revolution of one sort or another you may be holding worthless paper. It is up to the individual to assess the risk.

There is a very marginal rise in the interest rate of these bonds, because of the perceived slightly higher risk.

Derivatives

Derivatives markets will trade in various things that depend on or derive from, an underlying security inherent in that 'thing'. This security will determine the price of the investment. Basically, there are financial products derived from other financial products. The term 'derivative' is usually taken to cover futures, options and swaps. There are many other complex instruments, some of which are detailed below.

Futures

Futures contracts in the financial markets are generally used by companies and investors in order to protect themselves. The risk will be 'hedged' or offloaded. For example, a business exporting to another country can shield itself against currency fluctuations by buying 'forward' currency. That provides the right to have a currency at a specific rate at a specific date, so that any income from overseas sales can be more accurately predicted. A futures contract will bind two sides to the agreement to a later transaction, whatever it might be. It is a specific obligation set out to buy or sell an agreed investment or product at an agreed date. For example, an investor decides to buy a futures contract of £10,000 (whatever it might be for). It costs only 10% margin, in this case £1000. Six months later the price has increased to £15,000, so the investor can sell at a £5,000 profit. The opposite can be true with any investment, the price can go down as well as up. Futures contracts can be sold before the maturity date and the price of the contract will depend on the price of the underlying security.

There is also something called an 'index future' which is an outright bet, similar to backing a horse or other bet, with the money being won or lost depending on the level of index at the time the bet matures.

An extension of this is 'spread betting' which most people have heard of but do not understand. The spread betting company. for example will quote a company's shares at 175-200p If you think that the shares will rise by more than that you 'buy' at 175p in units of £10. If you are right and the price goes up to 210p the shares have appreciated by 10p and you have made a profit on your investment. However, if the share price falls then you have made a loss. If the price remains within the same price range then no one wins. Only a small amount of money is paid at the time the contract is made, so the potential profit margin is geared up. This is helped by the absence of capital gains on the proceeds, because it is a bet. This activity, spread betting, is a fast growing activity.

However, as with all betting, many people have lost a lot of money and warnings have been issued by the Financial Ombudsman and Financial Conduct Authority. My own advice would be don't touch spread betting if you have a limited knowledge of the financial markets and of share movements.

Forward contracts

As we have seen, a futures contract is an agreement, about commodities, currencies and financial instruments. Two sides to the contract agree to do a deal at some time in the future. A forward contract is a deal there and then, but for a future delivery. The contract is at a 'spot' price (the price currently prevailing) with a specified date for completion when the goods arrive.

Options

Options provide the right to buy or sell something as opposed to obligations contained within a futures contract. Someone for example, might option film rights for a future date. In relation to shares, buying a 'put' option, as it is known conveys the right to sell a set parcel of shares (usually 1,000) at a specified price at an agreed time. Because the price has been fixed at that time if the share price has fallen then the investor can make a profit. And, once again, vice versa. The opposite of a 'put' option is a 'call' option where the investor has the right to buy shares at a fixed price in the future. A profit is made if the shares rise substantially in the interim period. If they fall, a loss is made. All that has been lost is the margin of option money.

Options can be traded before maturity. This is known as 'hedging' ones position. For example, if someone knows that they will need funds in a few months time, to fund an acquisition, then if there is a worry that the market may fall in those months, then this is a way of buying protection: buying a put option at roughly today's price.

A basic example is if a company's shares are standing at 65p, it could cost, for example 6p to establish the right to buy shares at that price over the next three months. If the shares go up to 95p in that time then the investor can buy and sell immediately and make a profit of 24p. Like all our other examples there is a downside. If the shares fail to rise above 65p then a loss of 6p has been made.

The situation works the other way as well. If there is a suspicion that a company is about to lose serious value then someone can buy a put option-the right to sell the shares at a specified price- within an agreed set of dates. These rights have a value as well, related to how the share is performing and how long they have to run, so they can be traded, mostly on the London International Futures and Options Exchange

(Liffe) (part of Intercontinental Exchange Group now known as Euronext.liffe).

Covered warrants

Covered warrants are fairly recent. They are a more flexible option which is easy to deal with. They originated in Germany in 1989 and are very popular indeed. A covered warrant is the right to sell or buy an asset at a fixed price called the exercise price up to a specified date called the expiry date. This expiry date is anything from three months to five years at issue. The warrant can be based on a whole host of financial instruments or commodities. As with other derivatives investors can use covered warrants to gear up their speculation, as a way of hedging against a market change or for tax planning. Covered warrants are issued by banks or other financial institutions as a pure trading instrument. Covered warrants can be American (exercised at any time before expiry) or European (exercised only on specified date). If a warrant is held to expiry then it is automatically bought back for cash with the issuer paying the difference between the exercise price and the price of the underlying security.

A covered warrant costs less than the underlying security: this provides an element of gearing so when the price of the underlying security moves, the price of the warrant moves further. Warrants are a riskier purchase than the underlying security. A relatively small outlay can produce a large exposure and that makes warrants volatile. They can produce a large return or lose the complete cost of the warrant price, called the premium.

Overseas shares

As with major U.K companies quoted on the stock exchange in London, there are a number of large European and other companies listed. Most of them trade in the U.K so it is possible to get a clear idea of the business patterns and also to invest in them. The merger of European stock markets has made it relatively easier to gain access to overseas shares. There are a large number of internet based stockbrokers in Germany, France and Holland which make the task easier. You can buy overseas shares through a U.K. based stockbroker, however only a few offer such a service.

If you intend to purchase shares in overseas companies then it is very wise, as with all other share purchases, to carry out some research. There are added levels of risk with overseas shares in that information concerning important variables such as interest rate movements and the economy as a whole, plus the state of particular sectors may not be readily available whereas information concerning the U.K economy is and the overall level of knowledge is greater.

In addition to the above, there is the exchange rate risk. Profits from share trading overseas may be affected by movements in exchange rates.

As you can see, companies, although essentially easy to understand, operate in a market place where the range of different types of borrowings can get very complex. The next area of activity to understand if you intend to invest in shares is the medium through which shareholders, or would-be shareholders, purchase shares, that is the stock market.

****

SECTION 3.

OPTIONS FOR PURCHASING

SHARES

Ch. 7

Vehicles for Buying Shares and The Costs of Investing

Traditionally, shares were bought and sold through established means, such as investment companies and the various funds such as Hargreaves Lansdowne and A.J. Bell. However, with the growth of internet trading and 'share apps', it is much easier for individuals to make their own trades at a lower cost, in some cases for free. One thing is true though: it is just as easy, if not easier, to lose money as it always has been. We will be discussing the various vehicles for buying shares, including the best buy apps as we progress through the next two chapters. Chapter 8 deals specifically with internet broking and the various apps which also allow you to buy from your mobile phone.

Investing

When considering the initial amount to invest in a parcel of shares, it is important to realise that the less you invest the higher the overall cost of shares, because of fees etc, and the more a share has to rise to make a decent return. It is for this reason that most people in an advisory capacity would say that £2,000 is the minimum that should be invested.

For safety the investment should be spread over a number of companies. The old adage 'don't put all of your eggs in one basket' rings very true here. A common portfolio for a small investor should contain at least 12 companies (but not more as the other factor is that the investor should stay in control of his or her investments). The main aim of all investing is to get a decent return with the minimum acceptable risk. If you own shares in one company then the risk and possibility of losing your money is greater than if the risk is spread.

It is a general rule that the lower the risk the lower the return. However, the converse holds true, the higher the risk the higher the return. For some people who invest in a single company the rewards can be big if the company does well. In truth what usually happens is that large investments in one company will not produce massive returns or result in loss of all ones investment.

The shares will usually carry on rising marginally in the longer term.

Buying through Investments Trusts-Purchasing unit trusts

There are benefits connected to the purchase of unit trusts and investment trusts as opposed to individual shares.

With trusts you get a spread of investments over a number of companies, cutting the danger of one of the companies going out of business.

Investment trusts

Investment trusts are companies that invest in other companies on behalf of investors. They are termed close-end funds because the number of shares on issue is fixed and does not fluctuate no matter how popular the fund may be. This sort of investment is convenient for small investors who do not have enough money to buy a lot of shares in different companies thereby spreading the risk. An investment trust will have its money spread across a lot of companies so problems with one company will usually be compensated by a boom in another company. Managers of investment trusts are professionals, so, at least in theory, they will do better than the average person. It is true to say that investment companies are as good as their managers so it is wise to pick a company with a good and known track record.

Most investment funds have a lot of money to invest and they will usually invest in blue chip shares, unless specifically set up to invest in a specific type of share.

The cost of the stockbroker is the same as it would be with other dealings and the government stamp duty and the price spread between buying and selling price remains the same.

Although investment trust managers do have a lot of say in the nature and type of investments, investors will also have some say in what goes on by buying the right investment trust shares. There are trusts specializing in the higher risk stock markets (called emerging markets); there are some investing in the Pacific Rim and some concentrating in Japan; some go for small companies and some specialize in Europe and the United

States and so on. The spread of investments can be very diverse indeed and managers of investment trusts tend to be more adventurous on the whole than managers of unit trusts.

Some trusts are split capital trusts which have a finite life during which one class of share gets all the income, and when it is wound up the other class of share gets the proceeds from selling off the holdings.

Trusts are quoted on the Stock Exchange so the share price can be tracked and also the asset value of the trust can be calculated. The asset value is comprised of the value of the shares that the trust is holding compared with the trusts own share price.

One main reason that many are priced differently than their real value is that major investing institutions avoid trusts. Huge pension funds or insurance companies do not have to buy in to investment expertise as they normally have their own experts. Therefore trusts are used mainly by private investors.

Unit trusts

Unit trusts have the same advantage of spreading risk over a large number of companies and of having the portfolio of shares managed by professionals. However, instead of the units being quoted on the stock market as investment trusts are, investors deal directly with the management company. Therefore the paper issued has no secondary market. The investor cannot sell to anyone other than back to the management company. The market is seen from the manager's viewpoint: it sells units at the offer price and buys them back at the lower 'bid' price, to give it a profit from the spread as well as the management charge. Many unit trust prices are published in quality papers.

These are called 'open-ended' funds, because they are the pooled resources of all investors. If more people want to get into a unit trust it will issue more paper to accommodate them. Unlike the price of investment trust shares, which is set by market demand and can get totally out of line with the market value the price of units is set strictly by the value of shares the trust owns.

Tracker funds

Tracker funds move with the main stock market index, in the U.K that is usually taken to be the FTSE 100. This type of fund is for the less adventurous investor who looks for a virtually risk free return.

Open-ended investment companies

Open Ended Investment companies or OEICs are placed midway between investment trusts and unit trusts. They are incorporated companies and issue shares, like investment companies. Like unit trusts the number of shares on issue depends on how much money investors want to put into the fund. When money is taken out and shares sold back, those shares are cancelled. The companies usually contain a number of shares segmented by specialism. This enables investors to pick the area they prefer and to switch from one fund to another with a minimum of administration and cost.

Advantages of pooled investments

Pooled investments reduce risk and are therefore a safer home for small investors. However, as they are safe they are unlikely to hit the outside chance of a high performer, as individual share speculators might.

As stated earlier, there are many different companies and a certain degree of research and knowledge is essential before committing. To be forewarned is to be forearmed. Quality newspapers will have regular league tables of performance. Be careful too with tables that are published showing performance. Obviously, tables can only look backwards to demonstrate past performance and it is the future that matters.

Trusts can do very well, but it may be that they have done well in a sector that has expanded and is now contracting.

Management charges for both investment trusts and unit trusts are usually high. One way of avoiding high charges is to opt for a U.S. mutual fund, which is the same as a unit trust and which has lower charges.

There is also the alternative of setting up your own investment vehicle which has become quite popular over the years. Investment clubs, described below, already very popular in the United States are growing more popular up in the U.K.

Basically, a group of people together pool cash for investment in the stock market. The usual way is for each member to set aside a regular amount each month and decide where to invest it. This has the advantages of avoiding charges, spreading investments and also the social spin off. Also, the work of researching shares is spread amongst members.

Exchange traded funds

Exchange-traded funds, or ETFs, are investment companies that are legally classified as open-end companies or Unit Investment Trusts (UITs), but that differ from traditional open-end companies and UITs in the following respects:

- ETFs do not sell individual shares directly to investors and only issue their shares in large blocks (blocks of 50,000 shares, for example) that are known as "Creation Units."
- Investors generally do not purchase Creation Units with cash. Instead, they buy Creation Units with a basket of securities that generally mirrors the ETF's portfolio. Those who purchase Creation Units are frequently institutions.
- After purchasing a Creation Unit, an investor often splits it up and sells the individual shares on a secondary market. This permits other investors to purchase individual shares (instead of Creation Units).
- Investors who want to sell their ETF shares have two options: (1) they can sell individual shares to other investors on the secondary market, or (2) they can sell the Creation Units back to the ETF. In addition, ETFs generally redeem Creation

Units by giving investors the securities that comprise the portfolio instead of cash. So, for example, an ETF invested in the stocks contained in the Dow Jones Industrial Average (DJIA) would give a redeeming shareholder the actual securities that constitute the DJIA instead of cash. Because of the limited redeemability of ETF shares, ETFs are not considered to be—and may not call themselves—mutual funds.

An ETF, like any other type of investment company, will have a prospectus. All investors that purchase Creation Units receive a prospectus. Some ETFs may furnish an investor with a summary prospectus containing key information about the ETF instead of a long-form prospectus. If an investor receives a summary prospectus, the ETF's long-form prospectus will be available on an Internet Web site, and an investor can obtain a paper copy upon request and without charge. Some broker-dealers also deliver a prospectus to secondary market purchasers. ETFs that do not deliver a prospectus are required to give investors a document known as a Product Description, which summarizes key information about the ETF and explains how to obtain a prospectus. All ETFs will deliver a prospectus upon request. Before purchasing ETF shares, you should carefully read all of an ETF's available information, including its prospectus.

The websites of the New York Stock Exchange and NASDAQ provide more information about different types of ETFs and how they work. An ETF will have annual operating expenses and may also impose certain shareholders fees that are disclosed in the prospectus.

Investment clubs

Investment clubs are an alternative to funds managed by professionals and as a result can keep costs down. Investment clubs are a group of private investors who pool their money and decide collectively how it should be invested. There are now well over 12,000 investment clubs in the U.K (2021). The ideal number of people in an investment club is usually between 4-20. If the membership exceeds 20 then HMRC will term the club a corporation and corporation tax will be payable. There are several stockbrokers, including major banks who have ready-made packages for investment clubs, such as Barclays and Nat West. There is a specialist charity called pro-share www.proshareclubs.co.uk which publishes a handbook on how to start an investment club. The advice contained in this handbook is very useful indeed because, although it is not absolutely necessary to have an in-depth knowledge of the stock market when joining an investment club it is at least useful to know something about the different sectors that you will be investing in.

For investors clubs there are model rules and constitutions that need to be adopted. As with all collective endeavours, from residents associations to enthusiasts clubs, rules and guidelines are essential. Investment club rules will set out, for example, how members can join and leave the club, a unit valuation system that is to be adopted, the decision making process, levels of monthly subscription, meetings, appointment of officers and so on. It is of the utmost importance that procedures are followed as disaster will almost certainly ensue. It is important to look at whether the club will run indefinitely, accumulating a portfolio or whether it has a specific life, say 5 years. An investor might be invited to join an existing club so it is important that these rules are already in place and that they are the right ones for you.

A few other tips: only join in with people that you like and trust. Ensure that their objectives and goals are the same as yours or it could end in tears later down the line. The criteria for choosing investments varies widely from club to club but many will go for the riskier end of the market because the club membership is additional to a members own personal investments. Some investment clubs will go beyond the stock market and invest in property either directly or indirectly through another vehicle.

The main advice given to any club member or would-be member is not to invest in anything that you do not understand. Avoid the overly complex and riskier markets such as derivatives, unless you have an expert on board. Most clubs invest a small sum, it could be under £80 per month, so this type of investing is just as much fun, and social, as it is serious money making. There are some investment clubs who have had runaway success but, on the whole it is for the smaller investor with other aims in mind.

The cost of dealing in shares as an individual

Share dealing can be expensive, particularly in Britain. It is the case that it is more expensive here than in many other countries, and also the whole process is more complex, at least for individual shareholders. True, there have been moves by high street banks and other companies to make the process more transparent but it is still the case that small shareholders find the process rather confusing. It is also the case that small shareholders are still perceived to be a nuisance, because they deal in small amounts of money which cost just as much to transact as larger deals.

Commission

Commission paid to stockbrokers constitutes the main cost of dealing in shares. Commissions vary depending on the nature of the work and the type of broker.

Rates of commission can vary anything from £5 per transaction up to £20 with commission on a sliding scale above the minimum depending on the value of the transaction. An order of £2,000 might cost 1.5%, with the rate falling the higher the transaction. There can also be a one-off charge of at least £10 for joining Crest, the UK stock exchanges registry of share holdings.

There are several internet sites, such as www.fool.co.uk which provide information about brokers commissions. It is worth looking at this site before going ahead.

The spread

As well as brokers commission there is the cost of trading. Shares are like other commodities, the costs of buying and selling shares will differ. This difference is known as the 'spread'. Spread varies with risk. Big companies listed on the FTSE 100, such as Barclays, British Airways etc have huge market capitalisations and many shareholders with regular deals every day so would have a narrow spread of say 1-1.5%. A company with few shareholders and little trade would have a spread of up to 10%. The result is that for shareholders of small companies the shares have to rise even higher to realise a profit. There is lots of free advice concerning shares. However, it is true to say that for the small, first time investor even free advice can be confusing and misleading, given that this advice is often slanted in favour of whoever gives it. It is therefore advisable to use a stockbroker who is seasoned and knows the markets well.

For those with a larger share portfolio it is possible to sub-contract out the management. The stockbroker managing the portfolio will advise on investments but leave the final decision to the investor. The value of portfolios has to be high however, and this will not usually be the route for small investors. In addition to portfolio management there is discretionary management where a fee is paid to an advisor to provide advice on shares and also the timing of share purchase. The fee paid is quite high, or is based on a percentage and is therefore only useful for those with bigger portfolios.

Income tax

When you buy shares, you usually pay a tax or duty of 0.5% on the transaction.

If you buy:

- shares electronically, you'll pay Stamp Duty Reserve Tax (SDRT)
- shares using a stock transfer form, you'll pay Stamp Duty if the transaction is over £1,000

You'll have to pay tax at 1.5% if you transfer shares into some 'depositary receipt schemes' or 'clearance services'. You pay tax on the price you pay for the shares, even if their actual market value is much higher.

Transactions you pay tax on

You pay tax when you buy:

- existing shares in a company incorporated in the UK
- an option to buy shares
- an interest in shares, eg an interest in the money from selling them
- shares in a foreign company that has a share register in the UK
- rights arising from shares, eg rights you have when new shares are issued
- When you don't pay tax

You don't have to pay tax if you:

- are given shares for nothing
- subscribe to a new issue of shares in a company
- buy shares in an 'open ended investment company' (OEIC) from the fund manager
- buy units in a unit trust from the fund manager

You don't normally have to pay Stamp Duty or SDRT if you buy foreign shares outside the UK. But you may have to pay other taxes.

When you sell the shares
You may need to pay Capital Gains Tax when you sell your shares.

Buying shares
The process of buying shares has become markedly easier over the last few decades. In fact, many people have acquired shares through privatisations and through building societies becoming banks, and have not had to use a stockbroker. However, if people want to buy shares in the usual way there are several routes.

The first one is finding a stockbroker. Years ago, this was out of the reach of the small investor. Most stockbrokers operated within exclusive circles. Many did not want to be bothered with the small investor who knew very little, if anything about the markets. Banks have entered the arena with share dealing services and so has a new breed of transaction only brokers (who buy and sell but do not offer advice).

However, more and more information is becoming available, through the internet and in newspapers. There has been a trend to present information in a plain English way and the information regarding shares is no different. Finding a broker over the internet is probably the easiest way to get started.

The internet has undermined the closed nature of share dealing and there are a large number of independent companies, most of which are members of The Association Of Private Client Investment Managers and Stockbrokers (see useful addresses). Many have their own web sites.

There are three main types of broker, each offering a differing array of services: execution-only brokers; advisory brokers; discretionary brokers.

Execution only brokers

Execution-only brokers will simply handle the sale or purchase of shares at your request, whether this is carried out online or on the phone. They do not offer investment advice. The firms computer routes your order to the market where the shares are trading and it will simply execute your order at the best possible price. The broker will receive a commission on each transaction.

Advisory brokers

As the name suggests, an advisory broker will offer the best advice and strategies for you to increase the value of your investment portfolio and achieve your investment aims. This type of broker will try to get to know you and to gain a clearer idea of your aims. An advisory broker will be more expensive than an execution only broker, because of the more intensive nature of their service, but if you take advantage of the expert advice on offer then it will be worthwhile.

Discretionary brokers

This type of broker will have written authority from you or someone acting on your behalf to decide what securities can be bought and sold on your account.

For most new investors who may not be very knowledgeable about the markets or investing, it is generally safer to go with an advisory broker who can help you through the maze and also help to maximise the value of your investments.

People who think that they need help and advice can go to one of the big high street financial institutions with branches round the country. They can also seek out a good local firm that is experienced in the needs of small investors. The best way to find such a firm is by recommendation (like a lot of things) or you can go to the Association of Private Client Investment Managers and Stockbrokers.

Before picking a broker, ask questions such as how easily contactable are they and other terms and conditions.

In the next chapter, we look at the process of the individual buying and selling shares over the internet, which has become more and more popular over the last ten years or so.

Ch. 8

Internet Broking

Internet broking has, like many other activities on the internet, grown massively. The internet has a lot of real advantages. Investors can place an order whenever they feel ready and can do it from any place any time. In addition, an enormous amount of information is available online to assist with decision making.

Dealing on the internet can also be cheaper. It is possible to deal over the net for a flat fee of around £10, although this varies (see below). This is important for those who plan to be active investors and to whom the fees paid are crucial to profit margins. One Paris based research outfit called Blue Sky reckons that the four best value online brokers are all German.

The table overleaf shows 7 UK brokers with good reputations. However, there are many more brokers on the net and it is better to look around. Most banks, such as Barclays, have a share dealing service, with varied pricing.

See overleaf.

Name	Annual fee	Frequent trader rate	Charge per trade
Halifax www.halifax.co.uk	0.5%		£12.50
Hargreaves Lansdowne www.hl.co.uk		£5.95	£11.95
Iweb www.iwebb-sharedealing.co.uk			£5
Self trade www.selftrade.co.uk		£6	£12.50
AJ Bell You Invest www.youinvest.co.uk		£4.95	£9.95
Interactive investor www.ii.co.uk		£5	£9.99
Shard Capital www.shardcapitalstockbrokers.co.uk			Varies

However, you should check the online dealers and their charges regularly.

For a periodic update go to www.money.co.uk/investing. One acknowledged problem with the web is that it is hard to get a picture of the reliability of the firm that you are dealing with. The web is largely faceless so there are risks of various sorts, such as hacking into your data and so on. Online trading does not generate a share certificate. The shares are registered to the new owner but it is still computerised and the broker will hold the title to them in a nominee account. This can mean that the investor cannot easily change allegiance to another broker.

To join an online stockbroker, you need to get on to a website and follow instructions for registering. Almost all will require cash deposited with the brokerage. Interest is paid on this money at a low rate. When signing on you register a password which provides secure access for the investor.

United Kingdom brokers support Islamic accounts or swap-free accounts. United Kingdom Islamic accounts have no rollover interest on overnight positions to comply the Muslim faith. Traders of Islamic faith are forbidden to pay interest

If you want to invest in the US you might want to go through a US based broker. These brokers are cheaper than European counterparts.

There is a site that compares the overall performance of several online brokers, this is: www.europeaninvestor.com

There are two sorts of dealing online: one is to e-mail an instruction to a broker who will execute it via his trading screen. In theory he can do that within 15 seconds and within 15 minutes the deal can be confirmed. The other method is called real time dealing in which the investor connects directly to the stock market dealing system.

Normally, when the instruction is given, the broker will 'transact at best'-buy at the lowest available price and sell at the highest. The broker can be set a limit-the maximum at which you are prepared to buy or the minimum price below which you are not prepared to sell. Usually, such limits last for 24 hours although can be longer.

Once the transaction is complete the broker sends a contract note detailing the deal and how much money is to change hands. It may take some time to receive the share certificate but the important element is the presence on the share register.

A selection of share trading apps

Etoro www.etoro.com

eToro lets you buy and sell a range of financial instruments, including stocks, currencies, exchange traded funds (ETFs) and bonds without paying any commission. It has shares from the world's biggest stock exchanges and advanced charting tools. It's free to create an account, and there's no limit on how much you can trade.

Best trading app for mobile trading:

Fineco https://finecobank.co.uk

Fineco lets you access more than 26 markets worldwide and trade more than 20,000 financial instruments. It's pretty new for UK traders but is one of Europe's largest banks. Fineco lets you trade futures, stocks, currencies, bonds, exchange-traded funds (ETFs), options and funds. It has an advanced platform on offer with great charting tools and notifications. For beginners it's got free webinars, live events and videos to teach you all about share trading and keep you in the loop about what's going on in the stock market.

Best trading app for beginners: IG https://www.ig.com/uk

IG is an investing all-rounder - it's got an ISA, a pension and general investment account and offers ready-made portfolios, individual shares, contracts for difference (CFDs) and spread betting. This makes it suitable for everyone, from beginners all the way to experienced investors. Its platform goes into a lot of depth and with so many options it can be a bit overwhelming for beginners, but it has some great learning resources that are free to access, including a fantastic "IG Academy" which takes you through specific topics, with videos, guides and quizzes to help you learn.

Best trading app for range of features: Hargreaves Lansdown https://www.hl.co.uk

Hargreaves Lansdown is an all-rounder in the investing universe. It has an ISA, SIPP and junior accounts all on offer. It's more expensive than some providers, especially if you don't trade often, but in return you get a lot of information and guides that can help you make trading decisions. The Hargreaves Lansdown app lets you keep track of your investments from anywhere in the world.

Best trading app for investing in funds: interactive investor https://www.ii.co.uk

interactive investor offers nine different accounts including ISAs, pensions and junior accounts to help you manage you and your family's investments all in one place with one flat fee. You can invest in shares, funds, investment trusts, exchange traded funds (ETFs), venture capital trusts (VCTs), bonds and gilts. Interactive investor has a great fund offering, with nearly 3,000 funds available to invest in, a screener that lets you search for funds and get more information as well as lists of popular funds, news and insights.

Best trading app for international trading: DEGIRO
https://www.degiro.co.uk
DEGIRO lets you trade on more than 50 stock exchanges in 30 countries worldwide. It lets you invest in shares, bonds and ETFs, which can help you diversify across different financial instruments. It's worth noting that you can't invest in an ISA or pensions product with DEGIRO. It gives access to millions of shares in international markets. Mobile app that allows you to access your portfolio anytime and anywhere you are.

Best trading app for ease of use: Fidelity
https://www.fidelity.co.uk
Fidelity offers your typical stocks and shares ISA and self-invested personal pension (SIPP) as well as junior products, including a junior SIPP, if you're organised enough to pay into your child's pension. Fidelity's platform is the easiest to use of the platforms. It's got everything laid out well and an easy to use "step by step" approach,, instead of just throwing you in at the deep end. If you're a bit new to the investing game, then it gives you loads of options to invest based on your risk profile and your

investment goals, these allow you to try it out without the depth of knowledge that experienced investors have.

Trading 212 https://www.trading212.com

Trading 212 has all the tools you need to learn about trading and how it works. It's got a huge wealth of information on trading in the "learn" tab on its website, where you can find videos, guides and an alphabetical index to find out everything you ever wanted to know about share trading. On top of this, it has a great demo feature. This lets you trade with £50,000 in virtual funds to see more about how the platform works. Once you're ready to get started for real, you just hit "Real Money". You can trade more than 10,000 stocks and ETFs with Trading 212 and get access to 7 different markets. It's got access to some advanced charting tools in its desktop and mobile apps. Free to use – there aren't any fees for trading with Trading 212.

Best trading app for range of markets: Saxo Markets https://www.home.saxo

Saxo has a huge range of shares available from a variety of different stock exchanges, so you can invest in plenty of UK and overseas shares. It is an all-rounder platform, which means it's got all the products you'd ever need, including ISAs and pensions. Saxo is a great platform for experienced investors as it's got a nice range of tools, plenty of information and research, as well as webinars to help you find and research your investments.

How to choose the best trading app

There are loads of different things that you should consider when choosing the best trading app for you, such as:

- Fees and charges. Some platforms charge a flat fee, while others charge based on how much you invest.
- What you can trade. Such as shares, ETFs and funds.
- How easy the platform is to use. Some platforms are designed for more experienced investors, so might be quite complicated and difficult to use.
- Market research and tools. The tools available on the platform can be helpful in understanding your investments.
- Demo account. If there's a demo account available then you can give it a go without putting down any real money, this is a nice touch if you're new to investing.

Robot Fund managers

Robo advisors offer a digital, mostly app based investment service. Investors can set up accounts with as little as £1, make monthly contributions to their investments and access their cash quickly. The idea is that savers do not have to pay for financial advice to ensure that their nest egg is spread across stocks and bonds. Robo advisors ask a series of questions about your wealth, experience and risk tolerance before matching you with a diversified portfolio. The more low-risk you are the more bonds you hold.

Since the first app, Nutmeg was launched many companies have got in on the act. However, this route to advice has not proved that popular with investors choosing to go down the more traditional online broker route.

In the previous chapters, I have explained the workings of the Stock market and also how companies raise capital on the stock market. Also, we have looked at vehicles for investing in stocks and shares and also the costs of purchasing shares. In the following chapters we will look at the nature of information that is presented in newspapers, in particular the Financial Times, and how to interpret that data. Following that we will look at companies in more depth and then at the situation concerning share purchase, dividends and taxation.

****

SECTION 4

INTERPRETING FINANCIAL INFORMATION AND CHOOSING A SHARE

Ch. 9

Interpreting Financial Information-Reading The Papers

It is very important to be able to interpret the range of information about stocks and shares, and company information that is printed in newspapers each day. The frequency and extent of the information will differ slightly depending on the newspaper. In this chapter we will concentrate on the UK equities market as this is the area which most small investors will be interested in.

As we have seen, an equity is another word for a share or stake in a company. The owner of the share will, hopefully, receive a dividend annually and will enjoy capital appreciation. The equity markets in the UK trade shares across a wide range of companies, from established and stable blue-chip companies to the more high-risk ventures.

Although many newspapers do provide information concerning the equities market, and the information is the same, in this chapter we will concentrate on the best known paper dealing with financial information, the Financial Times, or FT. The financial times gives in depth daily coverage of the equities market and this consists of the following elements:

- A report daily of the most interesting trading features of the stock market.

- The share price of individual companies.

- Various financial ratios

- Reports on individual companies

- Stock market indices indicating overall progress of equity share prices.

The London Stock Exchange Market Information

The London Stock Exchange is just about the most comprehensive record of UK market statistics available to the general public and covers around 3,000 shares. The Market Share Service is divided into different industrial classifications.

The share service covers companies listed both on the main stock market and also the Alternative Investment market (AIM), discussed earlier.

The market information is published in the FT from Tuesday to Saturday in the companies and markets section. The table overleaf indicates the way the information is presented. Note that this is a representation only.

See overleaf.

Aerospace and defence

Notes	Price	Change	High	Low	Yield	P/E	Vol 000's
BAE Systems	229	-2.5	291.5	199.25	3.3	16.8	35.419
Chenning	490.5	-1	491.5	373.5	1.9	13.4	79
Cobham	1367	-32	1460	1237	2.3	14.5	370
Hampson	21.75	-1.5	30	18.25	-78.5	.5	262
Meggitt	297.5	-3.25	300.25	208	2.4	19.0	2756

The symbols below will be indicated alongside shares and can be interpreted as follows:

'**A**' alongside a share name indicates that it carries no voting rights.

♣ indicates that investors can get a free copy of the company's latest reports and accounts.

♥ this indicates that the stock is not listed in the UK.

♠ this indicates an unregulated collective investment scheme.

Xd means that the recently declared dividend will still be paid to the previous owner of the share.

Xr indicates the same for a rights issue- i.e. the buyer will not be acquiring the right to subscribe to the new issue of shares.

Xc means that the buyer does not get a scrip issue of shares which the company is issuing in lieu of a dividend.

Interpreting the figures

Interpreting the figures is largely self- explanatory.

1. The first column – notes - lists the company name.

2. The second column – price – shows the average (or mid price) of the best buying and selling prices quoted by market makers at the close of market on the previous day, the close being 4.30pm. If trading in the share has been suspended for some reason then this is denoted by a symbol and the price quoted is the price at suspension. The letters 'xfd' following a price mean ex-dividend and indicate that a dividend has been announced but this will not be available to new purchasers.

3. Price change. This will be plus or minus depending on the movement of the shares. This column will give the change in closing price compared with the end of the previous day.

4. Previous price movements. The fourth and fifth columns show the highest and lowest prices recorded for the stock during the past 12 months.

5. Dividend yield. The sixth column shows the percentage return on the share. It is calculated by dividing the dividend by the current share price.

6. Price earning ratio (P/E). The seventh column is the market price of the share divided by the companies earnings (profits) per share in the last 12 month trading period. Yields and P/E ratios move in opposite directions: if the share price rises, since the dividend remains the same, the dividend yield falls; at the same time, since the earnings per share are constant, the P/E ratio rises.

112

7. The last column, 8, deals with the number of shares traded the previous day rounded to the nearest 1,000.

How to use the information effectively

The first indicator to look at is that of price. The price is the current price of a share. This needs to be looked at in conjunction with the 52 week high and low in order to get some kind of historical perspective of performance of the company.

The prices quoted are the mid-prices between the bid or buying price and the offer or selling price at which market makers will trade. The difference between bid and offer is known as the spread and it represents market makers profit on any given transaction. The implication of the spread is that investors will only be able to buy at a higher price and sell at a lower price than that quoted in the newspaper.

Volume is an indication of the liquidity of a stock, or how easy it is to buy and sell. High volume is much more preferable than low volume but take into account the fact that smaller companies are traded much less heavily than larger companies. Volumes will also be higher when a company makes an announcement. The dividend yield is a reflection of the way that the market values a company. If the company is thought to have a high growth rate and is deemed to be a secure business, then its current dividend yield will be low, since the scope for increasing dividends in the future is average.

The dividend, to some degree, is an arbitrary figure, decided at the whim of a company. The figure for the yield is not always a good indicator of the vale of a share. Price/earnings ratios are generally better as they are independent of arbitrary corporate decisions.

Price/earnings ratios are the most commonly used tool of stock market analysis. Essentially, they compare a company's share price with its annual earnings, indicating the number of years that it would take for the company, at its current earning power, to earn an amount equal to its market value. Shares are often described as selling at a number times earnings or on a multiple. In general terms, the higher a company's ratio the more highly rated it is by the market. High price/earnings ratios are usually associated with low yields.

A high ratio suggests a growth stock and is, like a low yield, an indicator of an investment where capital growth might be more important than income.

Evaluation of weekly performance

Monday's edition of the financial times will indicate weekly changes in share prices. The column will look as follows:

(Overleaf)

Weekly tables

1	2	3	4	5	6	7	8
Notes	Price	WK% Change	Div	Div Cov	Mcap £m	Last XD	City line
BAE Systems	♣288.25	4.3	9.5	1.8	9,262	20.4	1890
Chenning	476.5	1.3	9.4	3.9	138.6	11.5	2116

The weekly column indicates:

1. Notes-the name of the company
2. Price with relevant symbol
3. The weeks price change as a percentage
4. Dividend – the dividends paid in the last financial year
5. Dividend cover - the ratio of profits to dividends, calculated by dividing the earnings per share by the dividend per share. This indicates how many times a company's dividend to ordinary shareholders could be paid out of net profits
6. Market capitalisation – this is an indication of the stock market valuation of the company in millions of pounds. It is calculated, as we saw earlier, by multiplying the numbers of shares by their market price.
7. Ex-dividend date – this is the last date on which a share went ex-dividend, expressed as a day and month unless a dividend has not been paid for some time. On and after this date, the rights to the last announced dividend remain with the seller of the stock. The share register is frozen on the xd date and the dividend will be paid to the

people on the register at that time. Until it is paid, buyers of the share will not receive the next payment due.

Other share dealings

Financial times share price coverage is expanded on a weekly basis on ft.com to cover dealings in securities that are not included in the standard share information service. Information is provided on name and stock type plus price.

Trading volume

The back page of the companies and markets section has a useful reference table with the trading volume and basic price information for the constituents of the FTSE Index, the index of the top 100 UK companies. This will deal with the largest capitalised and most actively traded stock.

Trading volume, price and change in stocks are indicated in this table. Trading volume is an indication of the liquidity of a stock. The higher the figure, the easier it will be to buy or sell significant quantities of stock without having a major impact on its price.

The FT carries three other lists for quick reference on share price movements.

Share rises and falls

This table, shown daily, shows how many securities rose, fell and stayed at the same price level during the previous trading session. It is broken down into nine different categories of security and shows how movements in the main share price indices were reflected in trading across the various market divisions.

Highs and lows

This table shows which shares have, on the previous day reached new high or low points for the past 12 months. The highs and lows table highlights company's that are moving against the general trends of their sector.

Main movers

This table will indicate the stocks that had the biggest percentage rise and falls the previous day. It will indicate the name of the company, the closing price, the days change as a price and percentage.

Winners and losers

Saturday's FT includes a table of the FTSE winners and losers. This lists the top and bottom six performing companies over the previous week in three sectors (the FTSE 100, the FTSE 250-350 and the FTSE SmallCap sector, 351st-619th companies). Included will be their latest price, percentage price change on the week and change on the start of the year. It also lists the six top and bottom performing industry sectors.

There are price tables for unit trusts and gilts. Gilts are normally split into short, medium and long-dated. There are also two undated ones and index-linked stocks. Foreign governments also issue bonds that are listed.

Indices

Newspapers also print information for the movement of specific industrial sectors, plus some describing the type of share. These are then aggregated to form wider industrial indices such as Basic Industries, General Industrials, 650, All Share and so on. The Financial Times produces a full list of the FTSE indices compiled and calculated under formulae developed by actuaries.

Every stock market has its indices to show movements in the market as a whole. Different papers report different selections of these. As mentioned previously, some of the better known ones are the Dow Jones, Nasdaq, Standard and Poor's, Toronto 300. Nikkei, Hang Seng, Dax for Germany, CAC40 for France and the Toronto Composite Index. There is also a table for the highest volumes of trade.

Papers such as the Financial Times will also provide invaluable editorials and views of experts which should be studied carefully as they are quite often right and can steer investors away from potential problems.

Having looked briefly at the presentation of information, and how to interpret that information, we will now examine two models of analysing a share, Fundamental and technical analysis. These two models help investors make up their minds about where to invest. They are simpler to understand than their names suggest.

Eurotop

The Times Newspaper is a good place to look for the top 100 shares in Europe. Similar to the FT breakdown the list will show closing price, percentage change, 12 month high, 12 month low, yield and P/E. A sample of the layout is below.

Eurotop	Close	%	12 Month high	12 Month Low	Yield	P/E
RWE AG	31.98	+0.76	31.98	21.04	2.30	
Swatch Group AG	260.00	+0.50	322.00	247.70	3.15	16.45
AP Muller –Maersk A Do Kr	8150	+145	9825	6355	1.99	26.37
AP Muller –Maersk B Do Kr	8622	+180	10555	6716	1.88	27.89

****

Ch 10

Choosing a Share

The collective price movement of shares is widely viewed as a leading economic indicator. It is believed to indicate strongly which phase of the business cycle - i.e. expansion, prosperity, recession and recovery-the overall economy is headed towards. For example, when stock prices are moving lower and lower despite occasional rallies, it could indicate that business profits will be slowing in the future, which could turn the economy into a recession. Conversely, if stock prices begin to show an overall upward trend, it could be a sign that the economy is heading towards a recovery.

Following on from the above collective analysis, there are two approaches to analysing shares for investment: fundamental analysis and technical analysis. Although fundamental analysis and technical analysis are quite different, many investors combine aspects of the two to help affirm or give support to a particular outlook about an individuals stock performance or the movement of the overall market.

Fundamental analysis

One approach to analysing shares for investment is that of fundamental analysis. This looks at the business and products of a company and also looks at its accounts, examining earnings and prospective dividends. Other factors such as the economy are examined along with the rate of inflation, level of currency, consumer demand and interest rates. In addition, economic competitors are examined along with efficiency of management. The analyst will then decide whether the business is adequately or fairly valued by the market.

Fundamental analysis concentrates on the true value of the company and then checks whether the share price reflects the true value. Nearly all the calculations are done by published accounts. Accounts reveal a wealth of information other than basic economic information and can demonstrate whether or not a company is doing well and stable or whether it is heading for trouble.

For the private investor, the process of identifying companies that are undervalued and therefore worth investing in is daunting, given the amount of companies in the UK. Also, given the amount of stockbrokers in the UK most of the companies have been covered anyway.

For the private investor there are ways of spotting potential companies to invest in. The answer is to have a set of personal criteria within which you will act. You can stick to companies with a P/E (price to Earnings) ratio of no more than five or six, or with a yield at least 10% above the average. You can look at neglected sectors and try to analyse what the future trends are likely to be. Combine all the information to hand with other information such as consumer confidence, the state of the economy etc and this can provide the basis of a fundamental rational analysis.

There are five measures used in fundamental analysis that every investor should understand, regardless of the level of experience of the investor:

1. Earnings per share (EPS) and earnings growth

Most people analysing company performance firmly believe that a company's earnings are the central influence on the price movement of its ordinary shares. Investors buy or sell stock in anticipation of the company's current and future earnings.

Earnings are the portion of the company's turnover or gross revenues that remain after it has paid all operating expenses, bond interest and tax. the resulting net amount is the company's earnings after taxes. If the company has preference shares outstanding, the board will declare the fixed dividend on those shares. After the preference dividend is deducted from the earnings after tax, this leaves the company with the all-important earnings for ordinary shares.

The EPS are then calculated by dividing the earnings for ordinary shares by the weighted average of the outstanding shares during the period of time for which the earnings are being calculated. The formula overleaf demonstrates this:

(See overleaf)

Net income after taxes -

preference dividend

Earnings per share (EPS) = _____

Weighted average of

ordinary outstanding shares

A company may report its earnings in three ways: primary EPS, fully diluted EPS, or earnings before interest, taxes, depreciation and amortisation (commonly referred to as EBITDA).

Primary EPS. This earnings figure is calculated using as its denominator or divisor the weighted average of all ordinary shares outstanding in the stock market for the given earnings period, or the number of shares outstanding on the day at the end of the period when the calculation is done.

Fully diluted EPS. The calculation of this figure adds to the denominator the total of all the additional ordinary shares that would be outstanding if securities, such as convertible bonds, convertible preference shares, warrants and company issued stock options to management and employees were converted into outstanding ordinary shares.

EBITDA (earnings before interest, taxes, Depreciation and Amortisation). The advantage of EBITDA is that it reports the earnings figure before it is distorted by the creative accounting and other financial practices a company uses.

2. Price-Earnings ratio (P-E)

This ratio measures the market price of one ordinary share of a company's stock, relative to its earnings per share (EPS). the formula is simple:

$$\text{Price Earnings ratio (P-E)} = \frac{\text{Current market price}}{\text{Earnings per share}}$$

In simple terms, the P-E earnings ratio tells an analyst or investor how expensive a company's share price is compared to its earnings. If a more established company has a high P-E ratio compared to other businesses in the same sector, or in the overall stock market, this is interpreted to mean that the company's shares are overvalued-the share price is too high and likely to decline. Overall, a high P-E ratio is generally believed to be an indicator of volatility and risk. A low P-E ratio can be an indication that a company's stock price is too low. In short, the company is undervalued. A low P-E ratio is characteristic of companies in mature low-growth industries.

3. Turnover and profit

Turnover is the total amount of money coming into the company from its sales and other revenue sources before operating expenses and taxes have been deducted. Pre-tax profit is the remaining turnover after operating expenses and interest have been deducted. When evaluating turnover and profits in older, established companies, ideally you would like to see that both have been growing steadily over a number of years. Correspondingly, many younger companies in growth areas may not have profits or earnings as the company is investing any money it makes in new operations, such as research and development, hiring staff, marketing and so on.

There are other reasons for low profit, such as poor management of the company. It is absolutely necessary to have clear information about company performance before any conclusions can be drawn. The bottom line is that turnover and profit are the driving forces of a stock price's improvement.

4. Dividend Yield

Dividends are that portion of a company's earnings that its board of directors decides to pay to ordinary shareholders. Most companies declare and pay dividends semi-annually, although some large companies pay quarterly.

No company pays out all of its earnings as dividends. It retains part of the money (retained earnings) so that it can meet its financial commitments and also have spare cash for any opportunities that may arise.

$$\text{Dividend yield} = \frac{\text{Annual Dividend Amount}}{\text{Current market price}} \times 100$$

When the total annual dividend per share is divided by the share's current market price, the result is the dividend yield. It tells the investor what percentage the dividend represents of the share's current market price.

5. Know the business and quality of management

It is essential that an investor has some idea about a company, its performance and its management before deciding to invest. It takes people to run a business. This is one of the main reasons that some business are successful and other are not: the quality of decision making and the nature of individuals moving that business along. You should also understand something about the industry and how it makes money. All of this requires work and background research but it will make you a more experienced investor over time.

Technical analysis

In contrast to fundamental analysis we have technical analysis, also known as Chartism. This is concerned with the movement of share prices in the recent past to try to gauge how they will do in the future. technical analysis is also known as Chartism because different charts are used to carry out technical analysis. the main charts used are bar charts, line charts and moving average charts

Technical analysis ignores the underlying worth of the business. It is not concerned with efficient management but only when the market price is likely to change. The main point is to identify patterns and to deduce whether there is likely to be any significant movements.

Broad-Market indices

The four key broad-market indices that are followed daily and used as part of technical analysis are:

FTSE 100. This is the most widely published and quoted index for the UK stock market. It consists of the 100 largest UK-domiciled, blue chip, listed and traded companies on the London Stock Exchange (LSE) using criteria established with the Financial Times. (FTSE, the group that produces various indices, was a joint venture between LSE and the FT. It is now wholly owned by the LSE. The FTSE is a 'capitalisation weighted index'. This means that larger companies with the most outstanding shares (not including restricted stock - i.e. shares issued to management that have restrictions on how long they must be held and when they can be sold) at the highest price have the greatest influence over the index.

FTSE 250. Also, a capitalisation-weighted index, the FTSE 250 consists of the next 250 companies, by capitalisation on the London Stock Exchange that do not qualify for the FTSE 100 index in terms of size and liquidity.

The **FTSE 350** Index is a market capitalisation weighted stock market index incorporating the largest 350 companies by capitalisation which have their primary listing on the London Stock Exchange. It is a combination of the FTSE 100 Index of the largest 100 companies and the FTSE 250 Index of the next largest 250.

The FTSE 350 is not very widely followed. The terms "FTSE 350" or "FTSE 350 company" are however useful for referring to large listed British companies when one wishes to include companies outside the top 100.

FTSE All-Share. As the name denotes, this is an index of all company shares including those in the FTSE 100 and 250 indices, that trade on the London Stock Exchange. This capitalisation-weighted index is considered to be the broadest measure of the UK economy, representing 98% of total market capitalisation.

FTSE Small Cap. This index represents approximately 2% of the total capitalisation of the LSE and considers those listed and traded companies that are not included in the FTSE 100 and 250 indices.

FTSE has also created narrow-based indices that capture the performance of certain sectors, such as basic industries, consumer goods, information technology and financials.

Ethical investments

As we discussed in the introduction, in addition to the above ways of choosing a share to buy, ethical considerations come into play with an increasing number of investors. There are several arguments put forward in favour of ethical investments. The most common one is that it is the correct way to invest. If investment is carried out blindly, you could be in the situation where on one hand you might deplore a war or invasion but find out that you are in fact investing in a company that is manufacturing arms and selling them to the warring parties. Similarly, you might deplore the state of the environment but find out that you are investing in a company that is doing its share of raping the land.

Obviously, choosing a company is a matter of personal choice and so is the fact of drawing the line. Many companies have been shunned over recent years. In the bad old days of apartheid in South Africa, Barclays Bank was held up as a culprit as it conducted big business there. Tobacco companies have been shunned, oil, paper, timber (deforestation) mining, pharmaceuticals and so on. Companies have also been boycotted because of their negative polices on pollution, ozone depletion and waste management.

For the individual investor it is better to have a specific set of criteria within which to work as confusion can set in and probably rule out a vast number of companies, whose end business is making money. There are specific unit trusts that have been created to cater for ethical investors and many fund managers can point you towards one.

Sources of information for the small investor
Market signals

A sure sign that something might be up is when a company buys back its own shares. This is usually an admission of failure to manage. It shows that there are no more remunerative sources for the corporate cash in investing in the business. Either this, or the business is trying to boost its earnings per share figure without changing the fundamentals.

Director's dealings

Companies are obliged by law to inform the market about dealings in their shares by directors of the company. This will go out on the stock exchange news system. Directors may provide very plausible reasons for selling shares, but if this is the case then it is better to be cautious and find out what the situation is. Why did the director sell shares in his own company? It could be that money was needed but it is still better to find out.

Using stockbrokers to advise on shares

This might seem the obvious answer, to utilise experience. However, any investor needs to be up to date with the markets in order to understand the advice given to him by stockbrokers. This is because the advice given may not always be the best advice. Again, it is imperative to do your own analysis, both technical and fundamental, as outlined in this book, and not to jump in straightaway when a decision has been taken to buy shares. Look at all the factors, very subjective economic factors and also past and present performance before committing yourself. Read the newspapers, look at the figures and scrutinise the editorials so that you at least have a semblance of knowledge and can have a reasoned conversation with the professionals.

Questions to ask brokers

Whichever type of broker that you decide to use, there are basic questions that need to be asked, besides questions about their track record. Some of the questions that you may want to ask include:

- Do you handle orders for all the types of investments in which I am interested?
- What fees do you charge? How do you earn your compensation?
- Do you charge an administrative fee for keeping shares in a nominee account and other services such as handling dividends? What is the fee?
- Is interest paid on cash held in my brokerage account, if so what is the rate?
- How quick is your trade execution and reporting process? How soon is money released into my account after i have sold shares?
- What kind of online services do you offer?

Taking advice from a financial advisor or investment professional

Most people can plan their own finances, particularly by utilising information from newspapers and specialist magazines. However, a financial advisor is worth consulting if you need help in implementing a wealth building and investment programme. The first step is to find the right type of financial advisor. there is a crucial distinction between an Independent Financial Advisor

(IFA), who can recommend investment products offered by any company, and a tied agent who sells products on behalf of a single company. By definition, the independent advisor will offer more impartial advice than the tied broker. You need to ascertain how the advisors get their fees. Here are some key questions to ask a prospective advisor:

- What areas do you deal in, do you deal in all areas of financial advice such as retirement savings, savings etc?
- What will your fees be, including any initial charges and ongoing expenses?
- How long have you worked in this field?
- Have there been any complaints about you? (The FSA website will give details if there are any.
- What licences do you have? Which professional organisations are you a member of?
- How frequently will you provide me with written reports? can I contact you by phone with any questions or concerns that I might have?

As a footnote, there were radical changes to financial advice, to the way advisors earn their fees, which came into effect on 31st December 2012, under the Retail Distribution Review. Under this review, advisors are not allowed to accept commission payments from firms such as fund managers and insurers for selling their products. Instead, they have to charge clients fees that have been agreed upfront. There are two types of commission paid to advisors by fund managers, which you the investor end up paying. The first is an initial commission and the second is what is known as Trail Commission.

Trail Commission

Trail commission is taken out of the annual management charge (AMC) which is deducted from the clients fund every year and paid to advisors, even if they are no longer offering an active service.

While trail commission was banned on new investments after 31st December 2012, existing prior arrangements will be allowed to continue. Almost 90% of investors do not know what trail commission is, according to Investsmart. One advisor has admitted that it takes almost £6 million a year in 'legacy' trail commissions from clients to which it no longer gives advice. A £50,000 investment over 20 years will pay almost £9,000 to your advisor, according to calculations by the website Candidmoney.com.

Cost of advice likely to rise

Under the new regime, advisors can charge an hourly rate, a set fee according to the work involved, or a percentage of the money invested. In addition, you may have to pay VAT on the advice you receive. This will depend on the type of advice. If you wish to buy a product, for example, if you have an inheritance to invest or want to start saving for a pension then the advisors charges will be exempt from VAT if you then decide to go ahead.. However, if you approach the advisor without the intention of buying an investment product, for example if you simply go for an annual review of your portfolio, then VAT at 20% will be payable. If you are looking for a financial advisor the website unbiased.co.uk will help you find advisors in your areas, listing their qualifications and any areas of expertise. **Vouchedfor.co.uk** allows consumers to rate advisors applauding the best and naming and shaming the worst, based on quality of advice, service and cost.

If you feel that you have been in any way mistreated by your advisor you have the right to complain and seek action. You should start by writing to the advisor directly and if you don't receive an appropriate remedy use established procedures to lodge your complaint. If you are still not satisfied having exhausted all internal procedures then you should complain to the Financial Ombudsman Service (www. financial-ombudsman.org.uk). The FCA (Financial Conduct Authority) outlines the steps for making a complaint at its website www.fca.org.

The FCA also produces a leaflet called Guide to making a Complaint which they will send to you if you phone 0800 111 6768.

In the next chapter, we look at the all-important area of taxation-having made your profits how much do you give to the government. Everyone's favourite topic!

****

SECTION 5

SHARES AND TAXATION

Ch.11

Shares and Taxation

We talked about tax on shares in a previous chapter. The area of tax and share dealing has always been a bone of contention. However, it is an important area and must be understood.

Tax on shares

When you buy shares, you usually pay a tax or duty of 0.5% on the transaction. If you buy:

- shares electronically, you'll pay Stamp Duty Reserve Tax (SDRT)
- shares using a stock transfer form, you'll pay Stamp Duty if the transaction is over £1,000

You'll have to pay tax at 1.5% if you transfer shares into some 'depositary receipt schemes' or 'clearance services'. You pay tax on the price you pay for the shares, even if their actual market value is much higher.

Transactions you pay tax on

You pay tax when you buy:

- existing shares in a company incorporated in the UK
- an option to buy shares

- an interest in shares, for example an interest in the money from selling them
- shares in a foreign company that has a share register in the UK
- rights arising from shares, for example rights you have when new shares are issued

When you do not pay tax

You do not have to pay tax if you:

- are given shares for nothing
- subscribe to a new issue of shares in a company
- buy shares in an 'open ended investment company' (OEIC) from the fund manager
- buy units in a unit trust from the fund manager

You do not normally have to pay Stamp Duty or SDRT if you buy foreign shares outside the UK. But you may have to pay other taxes.

When you sell the shares

You may need to pay Capital Gains Tax when you sell your shares. See further on.

Buying shares electronically

You'll pay Stamp Duty Reserve Tax (SDRT) if you buy shares electronically through the 'CREST' system (a computerised register of shares and shareowners). The tax is taken automatically when you buy the shares, so you do not need to do anything else about your tax. SDRT is charged at 0.5% when you buy shares electronically.

If you do not pay cash for your shares but give something else of value to buy them, you pay SDRT based on the value of what you gave. If you're given shares for nothing, you do not have to pay any tax.

Buying shares 'off-market'

You must also pay SDRT on 'off-market' transactions. This is when shares are transferred outside CREST.

How to pay

Tax is not deducted automatically when you buy shares off-market. You'll need to send HM Revenue and Customs (HMRC) a written notice with details of the transaction. If you do not pay on time, you'll be charged interest from the due date until the date you pay. You may also get a penalty.

Buying shares using a stock transfer form

You must pay Stamp Duty on your shares if:

- you buy shares through a stock transfer form
- the transaction is over £1,000

You pay 0.5% duty, which will be rounded up to the nearest £5. Example:

If you buy shares worth £1,050, you'll pay 0.5% on this amount which is £5.25. You'll round this up to £10 to pay in

Stamp Duty. For shares under £1,000, you will not need to pay anything. You can get a stock transfer form from:

- a broker
- a lawyer or an accountant who deals in shares

You can also download a stock transfer form from the internet. Send the transfer form to HMRC and pay Stamp Duty Send your stock transfer form to the Stock Transfer office within 30 days of being signed and dated. You cannot currently (as from April 21) post stock transfer forms because of coronavirus (COVID-19). However, check on this. If you only have a paper copy of your form, you need to scan it and send by email. You must also pay the Stamp Duty within 30 days of the stock transfer form being signed and dated.

Special share arrangements

You pay Stamp Duty Reserve Tax (SDRT) or Stamp Duty at 1.5% if you transfer shares into some 'depositary receipt schemes' or 'clearance services'. This is when the shares are transferred to a service operated by a third party (for example, a bank). The shares can then be traded free of Stamp Duty or SDRT.

Not all of these schemes work like this. Sometimes the higher rate is not charged and you pay Stamp Duty or SDRT in the normal way. Check the details of your scheme with your stockbroker.

Capital gains tax

You may have to pay Capital Gains Tax if you make a profit ('gain') when you sell (or 'dispose of') shares or other investments. Shares and investments you may need to pay tax on include:

- shares that are not in an ISA or PEP
- units in a unit trust
- certain bonds (not including Premium Bonds and Qualifying Corporate Bonds)

You'll need to work out your gain to find out whether you need to pay tax. This will depend on if your total gains are above your Capital Gains Tax allowance for the tax year.

When you do not pay it

You do not usually need to pay tax if you give shares as a gift to your husband, wife, civil partner or a charity. You also do not pay Capital Gains Tax when you dispose of:

- shares you've put into an ISA or PEP
- shares in employer Share Incentive Plans (SIPs)
- UK government gilts (including Premium Bonds)
- Qualifying Corporate Bonds
- employee shareholder shares - depending on when you got them

Work out your gain

You'll need to work out your gain to find out whether you need to pay Capital Gains Tax. Your gain is usually the difference between what you paid for your shares and what you sold them for.

Market value

In some situations you should use the market value of the shares when working out your gain. Do this if:

- you gave them away as a gift to someone other than your spouse, civil partner or a charity
- you sold them for less than they were worth
- you inherited them and do not know the Inheritance Tax value
- you owned them before April 1982
- you acquired them through certain Employee Share Schemes

If the shares were given or sold to you by someone who claimed Gift Hold-Over Relief, use the amount that person paid for them to work out your gain. If you paid less than they were worth, use the amount you paid for them.

Selling in special circumstances

There are special rules for working out the cost of your shares if you sell:

- shares you bought at different times and prices in one company

- shares through an investment club
- shares after a company merger or takeover
- employee share scheme shares

Jointly owned shares and investments

If you sell shares or investments that you own jointly with other people, work out the gain for the portion that you own, instead of the whole value. There are different rules for investment clubs.

What to do next
Deduct costs

You can deduct certain costs of buying or selling your shares from your gain. These include:

- fees, for example stockbrokers' fees
- Stamp Duty Reserve Tax (SDRT) when you bought the shares
- Contact HM Revenue and Customs (HMRC) if you're not sure whether you can deduct a certain cost.

Apply reliefs

You may be able to reduce or delay paying Capital Gains Tax if you're eligible for tax relief. When you know your gain you need to work out if you need to report and pay Capital Gains Tax. You may be able to work out how much tax to pay on your shares. You can use the online calculator if you sold shares that were:

- the same type, acquired in the same company on the same date
- sold at the same time

You can not use the calculator if you:

- sold other shares in the tax year
- sold other chargeable assets in the tax year, such as a property you let out
- claim any reliefs
- are a company, agent, trustee or personal representative

Reporting a loss

The rules are different if you need to report a loss. You can claim losses on shares you own if they become worthless or of 'negligible value' (for example because the company goes into liquidation). HMRC has guidance on making a negligible value claim.

Selling shares in the same company

There's a different way of working out your cost if you've sold the same type of shares in a company that you bought at different times. You'll usually need to work out the average cost of your shares and deduct this from what you got for them to work out your gain.

Example

You buy 100 shares for 80p each. The total cost is £80. You later buy 300 shares for £1.20 each. The total cost is £360. In total, you have 400 shares costing £440 - the average cost of each share is £1.10. If you sell 150 shares, the cost of the shares for your tax calculations is £165 (£1.10 multiplied by 150). Deduct this from what you sold the shares for to work out your gain.

If you bought new shares of the same type in the same company within 30 days of selling your old ones, there are special rules for working out the cost to use in your tax calculations.

Investment clubs

You work out your gain differently if you've bought and sold shares through an investment club. An investment club, as discussed in a previous chapter, is a group of people that buys and sells shares together on the stock market.

Work out your gain

You'll get a written statement of your gains and losses (an 'investment club certificate (PDF, 212KB)') at the end of each tax year from the person who runs the club, for example its treasurer. When you know your gain, work out if you need to report and pay Capital Gains Tax.

There are special rules if you make any losses.

Leaving an investment club

The club buys back your shares if you leave, and you need to include any gain or loss when you're working out if you need to pay tax. Take your share of any gains during your membership of the club, and deduct your share of any losses. Add any income from dividends you received (after tax). Add any other money you received from the club, and deduct anything you paid into it (for example a monthly amount to invest). Deduct the total from what you received from the club for your shares.

Transferring shares into the club
If you transfer shares you already own into the club, you're treated as selling them and you need to work out your gain.

If you run an investment club
The investment club treasurer or secretary should:

- divide any income, gains and losses between its members according to the club's rules
- give every member a written statement at the end of each tax year - you can use HMRC's investment club certificate (PDF, 212KB)
- keep records including members' income and gains
- arrange to buy shares from members who want to leave the club

If you're starting a new investment club, make sure it has a constitution and rules. Get legal advice from a professional if you need help.

Tax relief

You may be able to reduce or delay the amount of Capital Gains Tax you have to pay if you're eligible for tax relief.

Relief	Description
Entrepreneurs' Relief	Pay 10% Capital Gains Tax instead of the normal rates if you sell shares in a trading company that you work for and have at least 5% of the shares and voting rights (known as a 'personal company').
Gift Hold-Over Relief	Pay no Capital Gains Tax if you give away shares in a personal company or unlisted company - the person you gave them to pays tax when they sell them.
Enterprise Investment Scheme (EIS)	Delay or reduce your Capital Gains Tax if you use a gain to buy unlisted shares in companies approved for EIS.
Seed Enterprise Investment Scheme (SEIS)	Pay no Capital Gains Tax on a gain of up to £100,000 if you use a gain to buy new shares in small early-stage companies approved for SEIS.
Rollover relief	Delay paying Capital Gains Tax if you sell unlisted shares to the trustees of a Share Incentive Plan (SIP) and use the proceeds to buy new assets.

Shares are 'unlisted' if they're in a company that is not listed on the London Stock Exchange or a recognised stock exchange abroad.

Dividends

How dividends are taxed

You may get a dividend payment if you own shares in a company. In the March 2017 budget, the chancellor reduced the tax free rate from £5,000 to £2,000 commencing from April 2018. This is still current in 2021/22.

Above this current £2,000 allowance the tax you pay depends on which Income Tax band you're in. Add your income from dividends to your other taxable income when working this out. You may pay tax at more than one rate.

Tax band	Tax rate on dividends over £2,000
Basic rate	7.5%
Higher rate	32.5%
Additional rate	38.1%

HM Revenue and Customs (HMRC) has examples of how your tax is worked out if you're over the dividend allowance. Go to the website:

www.gov.uk/tax-on-dividends/how-dividends-are-taxed.

You don't pay tax on dividends from shares in an ISA. Dividends that fall within your Personal Allowance do not count towards the £2,000 dividend allowance.

How you pay tax on dividends

How you pay depends on the amount of dividend income you got in the tax year. Less than £2,000 you don't need to do anything or pay any tax.

Between £2,000 and £10,000

Tell HMRC by:

- contacting the helpline 0300 200 3300
- asking HMRC to change your tax code - the tax will be taken from your wages or pension
- putting it on your Self Assessment tax return, if you already fill one in
- *Over £10,000*
- You'll need to fill in a Self Assessment tax return. If you don't usually send a tax return, you need to register by 5 October following the tax year you had the income.

****

In Summary

Important points to remember when devising an investment strategy.

Having read through this book, hopefully you will have gained some knowledge about the stock market, investments generally, companies and those who buy and sell shares, the brokers.

It is very important that, before you begin to invest you should know the markets. Educate yourself about the workings of the markets, understand stocks and shares thoroughly and also understand the role of the participants and their charges.

Your portfolio

Whether you are new to investing or whether you are experienced, there is one important principle to bear in mind: never place all of your investments in one vehicle, don't put all of your eggs in one basket. The key to a healthy and balanced portfolio is diversification. Deciding how to diversify your portfolio is called 'asset allocation', i.e. where do you put your money, cash, bonds, stocks and shares and so on.

How many funds is too many?

Putting money into a range of different funds can help to spread risk and seek opportunities. That's because in owning different asset classes that behave differently during the market's ups and downs, a portfolio should weather market downturns better.

What's the right number of funds to hold? Owning too few funds means your money perhaps isn't diversified enough. Too many and your portfolio can mutate into an unwieldy mess. Overlapping is an important consideration when you start snapping up funds left, right and centre. If, for example, you invest in 20 funds, you could be holding as many as 1,000 different stocks and in this pool it's likely you will be duplicating some of your investments. You will probably end up with something akin to an overpriced tracker. There's no point paying for active fund management if you take this kind of route to investing. Especially because, after fees, it will probably under-perform.

You may be able to find out how much overlapping there is in your portfolio by using a tool on your platform. At Hargreaves Lansdown it's called Portfolio Analysis, and at AJ Bell You Invest it's called Portfolio X-Ray. This can help you to analyse the true contents of your portfolio, whether it's 5 or 15 funds. When it comes to finding that magic number of funds to hold, there's no one-size-fits all figure, it appears. A rule of thumb is that a beginner can start with just one fund with a level of risk that fits their appetite – maybe a broad global equity fund or even a multi-asset fund that invests in equities, bonds and perhaps property, gold and commodities. As you get more experienced and more comfortable making your own investment decisions, the number of funds will grow. Experts at Fidelity suggest that an experienced investor with about £100,000 needs between 10 and 15 funds. Others suggest that you can stretch to 20. Any more and a portfolio becomes unmanageable.

There are several popular models of asset allocation which are widely used in the financial world and they are described below.

The Age-Adjusted Mix (Variable)

This is a model that many people find easy to understand and use. Its formula is designed to change your investment mix from focussing on capital growth in your early years to a more conservative approach whose objective is preservation of capital as you grow older. The formula is:

100% minus your age = Percentage of assets invested in shares or fund that invested in shares

The remaining percentage would be invested in bonds (or a mixture of bonds and low risk cash). So, when you are thirty years old, 100% minus your age would result in an allocation of 70% of your investment money to equities and 30% to bonds. When you reach 50, you would have 50% in stocks and 50% in high grade bonds. You would adjust the percentage each year.

The Conservative or Balanced mix (40% bonds and 60% shares)

This allocation model has preservation of capital as one of its goals, hence the high percentage in bonds. It seeks to provide steady income from the interest paid on the bonds, while offering some opportunity for capital appreciation, depending on the types of stocks and shares in the portfolio. It is important to rebalance this allocation annually. If shares have grown in value you sell them and reinvest the capital gains in low risk stock. If bonds have outperformed stocks then you sell bonds and use the profits to buy shares.

Deciding on an asset allocation model or strategy will give you the broad outline of your investment plan. There are a few other useful tips below:

- Focus on a limited number of companies-make sure you have control over what you invest-if you choose dozens of companies it is likely that you will take your eye off the ball.

- Invest over a period of time-don't feel that you have to invest everything at once. A prudent approach is to invest modest amounts of money at regular intervals as the markets move up and down.

- Pay attention to market trends. A bull market is a period of investor optimism., a bear market is the opposite. be aware of the market and the right period to invest.

- recoup your original investment and let your profits run. Once your securities have increased in value, you may want to sell off enough to recoup the original amount that you invested and let your profits continue to make money for you.

- Learn from mistakes. Whenever you lose money on an investment, don't immediately reinvest the money. Take time to reflect and ask yourself what you can learn from your mistakes.

****

Glossary of terms

Alternative Investment Market – the area of the stock market for small companies or those too young to meet the requirements for full listing

Authorized share capital – the amount of shares that a company may issue

Bear market – a time of falling share prices

Bid – the price at which managers of unit trusts will buy back the units from investors, compared with the offer at which they sell units

Blue chip – a highly rated company and its shares

Bond – a tradable fixed interest security

Bonus issue – this is another name for scrip issue or the distribution of shares to existing shareholders at no cost to them

Bull market – a time of rising share prices

Common stock – American term for ordinary shares

Convertible – a class of paper issued by companies (such as loan stock or preference shares) that can be converted into ordinary shares at a preset price, on a set date

Coupon – the interest rate on a corporate bond

Crest – the stock exchanges electronic register of share ownership to replace paper certificates

Dividend – this is an amount of money paid out to the holders of shares, based on an amount per share

Easdaq – European Association of Security Dealers Automated Quotation System

Equities – ordinary shares

Ex-dividend – a share that is sold soon after a dividend being announced with the seller still getting the payment

Flotation – bringing a company to the stock market to get its shares publicly traded

FTSE 100 – the top 100 companies in the UK with the highest market capitalisation

Fundamental analysis – looking at the company behind the share. This is in contrast to technical analysis which looks only at movement in share prices

Gearing – a ratio of a company's borrowings to its equity

Gilts – short for gilt edged, the name used for government bonds

Hedging – protecting against a potential liability

Insider – someone with access to privileged information. It is illegal to trade shares when in possession of such knowledge

Issued share capital – these are the shares that a company has actually sold

Leverage – the American term for gearing

Liffe – London International Financial Futures and Options Exchange

Liquidation – the sale of an insolvent company's assets to pay creditors

Liquidity – a measure of how easy it is to trade shares. Also used to assess assets by how readily they can be turned into cash

London Stock Exchange – the largest stock exchange operating in Britain

Members – the shareholders of a company

Nasdaq – National Association of Securities Dealers Automated Quotation System. This is a New York based system with an emphasis on companies using advanced technology

Net asset value – all the assets of a company minus all its liabilities and capital charges

Ofex – a computerised stock market run by market maker P Jenkins, founded in 1995

Offer – the price at which managers of unit trusts sell the units to the public

Price/ earnings ratio - this compares the current price of the share with the attributable earnings per share

Put option – the right to sell a share at a set price within the period of the agreement

Registrar – the organization that maintains the record of a company's shares and their ownership

Rights issue – a way of raising money by selling more shares sometimes giving people who own shares the right of first refusal in proportion to the shares that they own

Seaq – this stands for stock exchange automated quotations and is the electronic system that displays the bid and offer prices for securities by market makers, together with the size of the parcel that they will deal in

Share premium – if the nominal value of a company's share is 30p but it issues them at 50p the 20p difference is in the books as the share premium account

Shareholders funds – the assets of a company minus its liabilities; since shareholders own the business what is left belongs to them

Spread – the difference between the buying and selling price of a share or other asset

Stockbroker – a professional dealer in shares who acts as an agent for the investor

Technical analysis – another name for a chartist way of looking at the market

Warrants – a type of investment allowing the holder to buy paper from the issuer at a fixed price sometime in the future

Yield – this is calculated by taking the amount of a dividend as a percentage of the current share price. If a share stands at 100p a dividend of 10p represents a yield of 10%.

****

Useful addresses

Association of Investment Trust Companies 24 Chiswell Street London EC1Y 4YY Tel: 020 7282 5555 www.aitc.co.uk

Wealth Management Association 22 City Road, Finsbury Square,London EC1Y 2AJ Tel: 0207 448 7100 www.thewma.co.uk

The Investment Association Camomile Court, 23 Camomile Street London EC3A 7LL Tel: 0207 831 0898 www.theinvestmentassociation.org

Chartered Institute of Taxation
30 Monck Street, London SW1P 2AP Tel: 0207 340 0550 www.tax.org.uk

Companies House
www.companieshouse.gov.uk

Financial Conduct Authority 12 Endeavour Square London E20 1JN Tel: 020 7066 1000 www.fca.org.uk

Financial Ombudsman The Financial Ombudsman Service Exchange Tower London E14 9SR Tel: 0207 964 1001 www.financial-ombudsman.org.uk

Financial Services Compensation Scheme,

10th Floor

Beaufort House

15 St Botolph Street

London EC3A 7QU

0800 678 1100

www.fcs.org.uk

London Stock Exchange, 10 Paternoster Square, London EC4M 7LS

020 7797 1000.

www.londonstockexchange.com

Nasdaq www.nasdaq.com

New York Stock Exchange www.nyse.com

****

Index